The Heart of Creation

The Heart of Creation

The Meditative Way

JOHN MAIN

Introduction by Laurence Freeman

CROSSROAD • NEW YORK

1989
The Crossroad Publishing Company
370 Lexington Avenue, New York, N.Y. 10017

Copyright © 1988 The Executors of John Main OSB
Introduction © 1988 Laurence Freeman OSB

Biblical quotations are taken from the New English Bible
© 1970 by permission of Oxford and Cambridge University Presses

Printed in the United States of America

Library of Congress Cataloging-in-Publication Data

Main, John, O.S.B.
    The heart of creation : the meditative way / John Main ;
introduction by Laurence Freeman.
        p.   cm.
    Reprint. Originally published: London : Darton, Longman and Todd.
    ISBN 0-8245-0957-9
    1. Contemplation.   I. Title.
BV5091.C7M27   1988
248.3′4—dc20   89-32856
                                                        CIP

To the extended community
of Christian Meditation groups
throughout the world.

Contents

Contents

How to Meditate

Sit down. Sit still and upright. Close your eyes lightly. Sit relaxed but alert. Silently, interiorly begin to say a single word. We recommend the prayer-phrase 'maranatha'. Recite it as four syllables of equal length. Listen to it as you say it, gently but continuously. Do not think or imagine anything – spiritual or otherwise. If thoughts and images come, these are distractions at the time of meditation, so keep returning to simply saying the word. Meditate each morning and evening for between twenty and thirty minutes.

Addresses of meditation centres:

Christian Meditation Centre
29 Campden Hill Road
London W8 7DX
England
Tel: 01 937 0014

The Benedictine Priory
1475 Pine Avenue West
Montreal H3G 1B3
Canada
Tel: 514 849 2728

Monastery of the Holy Spirit
24 Murray Road
Croydon
Melbourne
Victoria 3136
Australia
Tel: 613 725 2052

Hesed Community
3745 Elston Avenue
Oakland
San Francisco
California 94602
USA
Tel: 415 482 5573

Introduction

A great many people have come to know John Main since his death. This in itself has broken one of the assumed rules of publishing; that a writer's reputation tends to decline when he is no longer there to promote a book by his visible presence. The exceptions to this rule are the important writers, the ones who not only communicate a tradition but develop it.

With each new book of his teaching to appear, more people come to know John Main and it might be of value to say a word about his life – a life that has exemplary value as a parable of pilgrimage. He was born in London in 1926 into an Irish family, and his life is interwoven with the themes of prayer and communication. After the war, in which he served in Intelligence behind the front lines, John Main tried a religious vocation and studied in Rome for a couple of years but returned to read Law at Trinity College, Dublin. On graduation he joined the Colonial Service and was sent to Malaya. There, he learned to meditate with a Hindu monk and what he learned from this teacher of the inner life he would one day teach in the Church.

On his return to the West John Main lectured in International Law at Trinity College, Dublin. In 1957 he became a Benedictine monk in London and, when he explained how he prayed hoping to find an understanding of what he had learned in the East, he was advised to stop meditating because it was not part of the tradition. So, as he later described it, he went into the desert for several years but only so that when he did return to the path it would be 'on God's terms not my own'.

Some years later John Main re-read John Cassian, whose writings had deeply influenced St Benedict and indeed the whole western tradition, and within the fifth-century conferences John Main rediscovered the mantra. From this time on he grew in the conviction that here was a tradition of contemplative prayer that answered the Church's new vision of the holiness of the people of God. He returned to London where he started a small lay community at the monastery which rapidly became a centre for meditation groups teaching this way to people of every age, background and walk of life. In response to the needs of individuals and of new groups forming outside the Centre, he began to write and to record his talks. *Word into Silence* dates from this period and remains a classic introduction to Christian meditation.

In 1977 at the invitation of the Archbishop of Montreal and of Bishop Leonard Crowley, John Main started a small community in Montreal, whose central work and aim would be living the gospel through the practice and the teaching of meditation. From here his work began to reach across the world, and, before his death at the end of 1982, an extended community of meditators had begun to form, reviving the awareness of Church as a fellowship rooted in prayer and contemplative action. The vision that led to this as a reality is presented in *Letters from the Heart* and *The Present Christ*.

The Heart of Creation makes a new part of John Main's thought and spiritual teaching available. The talks were first given to meditation groups meeting each week at the Priory in Montreal. Using the tapes of these talks and other written material in his notes, I have edited them in a way which will, I hope, like the earlier *Moment of Christ* make the gift John Main had to share accessible to many more people than would ever have been able to crowd into the meditation room in the Priory where he was such a vital teacher of the way of Christ.

John Main knew that the primary process of transcendence is prayer. Like T. S. Eliot he saw that prayer is, 'more than an order of words, the conscious occupation of the praying mind, or the sound of the voice praying'. For him it was pure attention, in which the searchlight of consciousness is turned completely away from its own streams of thought, feeling or perception. But what do we turn towards? What image or belief do we fix our mind upon to overcome the fear of losing our self-consciousness, the 'growing terror of nothing to think about'? John Main is a teacher in the apophatic tradition of imageless, nonconceptual prayer. And so his answer is the full and complete *nothing* called poverty.

Pure prayer means the transcendence of all thoughts and images. Not looking at God, but into God. It means seeing God with the imageless vision of faith, which is the power (and gift) which realizes our union with Christ at prayer in us. We see God through his eyes when we stop trying to see him through our own inadequate vision. We know God with the mind of Christ when, by renouncing the great human gift of self-consciousness, our mind becomes one with his.

In a frenetic and nervous civilization such as we inhabit, saturated with image, idea and self-commentary, the apophatic wisdom becomes a life-nourishing stream of refreshment and hope. Its ideas are hope-filled. The world hungers to hear them repeated continually because it forgets their truth so quickly. They are the ever-blooming discoveries of the Christian contemplative tradition. John Main knew them as truths verified by his own experience.

A sign of his authenticity is that in proclaiming them he transcended his own experience. In the short chapters of this book you will not find the entries of a spiritual diary. Nor, in spite of his favourite symbol of prayer as a pilgrimage, will you find the log-book of his personal searchings. That is one form of spiritual writing, confessional and autobiographical, which has had a noble and enriching tradition and enjoys a flowering today. But there is another and more classical form, explanatory rather than descriptive, which does not so much describe a search as explore what has already been found. Of course, as St Bernard's 'holy curiosity' reminds us, to search is to find and to find is to search again. But there are different emphases in spiritual teaching. They share a common impulse, however, that calibrates their innate value. This value consists in the concern to put one's own inner life at the service of others, just as an active apostolate dedicates one's external resources. But John Main's concern was not to make his own experience a vicarious one for others. It was to guide and help others to their own discovery, their own unique and eternal enlightenment.

It is difficult for some to believe this spiritual altruism of others, especially during their lifetime. Scepticism thrives on the discovery of mixed motives. And, as motives are conditioned by the changing circumstances of a lifetime, it is difficult to assess their consistent purity before death completes the narrative form of a life. Authentic teaching is, however, grounded in authentic personality which, while remaining fallibly human, nevertheless manifests an unusually high degree of integrity. How do we know whether we should listen to a teaching that challenges us and calls us to discipline? Ideas alone may enthuse us but can lead only to further reflection not to deeper conversion. Personality alone can dazzle us but fail to evoke mature commitment.

In John Main the church and the world is fortunate to find a teacher of wisdom who possesses an authentic personality rooted in the lived experience of a consistent and evolving system of ideas. Where, in his lifetime, many found the teaching brought alive in his personality, others today will find his personality immanent in his teaching. Ultimately human freedom demands we trust ourselves. But to come to this we need to place trust in a teacher. This is the Christian tradition from the earliest times. Our world today is impoverished by a lack of authentic teachers and a dearth of wisdom. The call for this book has come from all those men and women throughout the world who have found in John Main such a teacher, and who have learned from him so that they can pass on the teaching to others. Over the past few years I have seen the fruit of John Main's wholeness in innumerable individuals and meditation groups, centres and networks which have flowered in proof of his belief that the contemplative experience evolves into the Body of Christ.

To be convinced of anything we need to believe in the integrity both of the teacher and of his ideas. And without conviction we are powerless to make meaning. John Main would like to convince us, above all, of an understanding of prayer. He would share his vision with us of prayer as an experience of total humanity, in undistracted and unrefracted communion with God. Not the God who has died for modern consciousness and has left so many with the false sense of the absence of faith. Not the God of battlefields and sugar-candy. But the God Jesus worships. The blurred, monistic image of God is drawn into clear focus for John Main, and his readers, by the Christian revelation of the God of three Persons. Our relationship with God, the basic relationship of life in which all ultimate, humanitarian values are rooted, matures through prayer. In Christian prayer this relationship, which is so vital for our relationship with ourselves and with others, escapes the melodrama of an imagined encounter between the human and divine ego. Enlightened by the Spirit to see the Son as the revelation of the Father, we enter the Christian experience of prayer. We are thus prepared to stop listening to ourselves, prepared for redemptive silence.

In silence, relating to God becomes more than thought, dialogue or contractual bargaining. We cease asking the questions that are unanswerable because they are wrongly put: all the 'whys' by which we try to put God in the dock. Instead of questioning, we awaken. As consciousness deepens, it also clarifies and expands. We awaken to see that we know God by living our life in the life that unites the three persons in one nature. We derive our life from the divine nature and for this reason we remain as much a mystery to ourselves as God does to us. But we are also other than God and so we can, and must, know ourselves. Our life and meaning is inseparable from God because we are not fully ourselves until we return to God from whom we have come into being. We must join our end to our beginning. Only then do we cease continually to die. Then we begin to taste life that is eternal. Eternal life is true meaning, and in prayer all this is accomplished, by realizing that everything that occurs between the beginning and the end also fits together. This is the harmony John Main sees as the fruit of prayer.

He therefore sees prayer as something far greater than what we do. For John Main, prayer in the light of the Christian mystery is essentially not 'my prayer' at all, but our entry into the prayer of Christ. Christ's self-transcendent human consciousness catches us up into the stream of its own completion. In death and resurrection, in ascension and glorification, Jesus has joined end to beginning. And in sending the Spirit, he had endowed us with his own divine meaning. We go with Christ to the Father because we go beyond Christ. The necessary extra dimension of consciousness, which allows the paradoxical to be personally verified and which gives infinite room for expansion, is the Spirit, the divine person we never see.

Say your mantra. In these three words John Main, with heroic simplicity, highlights a way of transcendence. He challenges his reader to a personal and experiential theologizing, to know God 'in your own experience'. The poetry and philosophy are reduced to an irreducible poverty. Belief, with its tendency to endless elaboration, is recalled to its home in faith. It is an abrupt challenge, a stark recall. But it is softened when we see that it is constantly repeated. The teaching is consistent, renouncing novelty but endlessly renewed. From whichever direction these pages approach the mystery of prayer, you will find the same simple and direct advice. With the light of your own experience you will see in each re-finding a greater depth, a fuller clarity, a more personal meaning. Experience is the teacher and for this teaching of meditation to find fruitful soil it is important that it is being practised.

John Main describes the commitment and discipline needed for this ongoing experience. But they are put before us as wonderful truths of liberation and fulfilment, radical not rigorist. The uncompromising simplicity is tempered by the awareness that the work of prayer is co-operative, the Spirit of God joining with our spirit. We are given as many chances as we need. In learning to say the mantra we learn great Christian truths from our own experience. We learn the relation between humility and self-knowledge. We learn what it is to be accepted and to accept unconditional forgiveness. In failing to succeed in saying the mantra simply and continuously, we gradually gain the wisdom to see unitively, beyond the duality of success and failure. As we learn to say it, experience authenticates it as a way of discipleship.

When you enter upon this discipline, as this book invites and encourages you to do, it is not long before you stop expecting instant results. You start seeing that to grow spiritually is to renounce acquisitiveness at every level. Meditation merges into the substance of daily life, no longer a technique but a way of living in faith. Because it is an act of transcendence practised at the centre of the person, meditation has a radiating influence all round the circumference. It is in the situations and responses of life that the fruits of this ancient and timeless prayer will be discerned. But as you discern them, you will be led to a simultaneous awareness that the centre of your being is being expanded. 'It is not I that live but Christ that lives in me'. What seemed like a pinprick of isolated identity dilates to invite us into a universe of being.

It is important to be prepared for the conviction you will meet in this book and throughout John Main's writings. Because we are more familiar with scepticism or the comfort of easily-won agreement, conviction can make us uneasy. In reading John Main you are being directly, though always gently, challenged. He will encourage you by showing that the reduction to poverty is not impoverishing. Wherever two poverties meet, enrichment is engendered. Human and divine poverty meet in Christ at the centre of every human person. And so, it is there we enter the kingdom that, through its realization in us, comes to earth.

True single-mindedness is expansive, not constrictive. The invitation to meditation does not entail the exclusion of anything that has meaning. Indeed it restores meaning to practices or words that have been depleted of it. It will help to remember, as you read on, that the author was a monk. His life was lived in the continuously enriching rhythm of scriptural and liturgical prayer. He shared that life with lay people, including many of the young who were estranged from religious traditions. He realised that meditation restores us to reverence, renewed by the truly spiritual.

When John Main was asked if he thought this was the only way of prayer, he replied that it was the only way he had found.

It was his manner of replying to another of those wrongly phrased questions. His life and the teaching with which he guided others showed that the 'only way' does not exclude other ways. No more does Christ negate manifestations of the Word of God outside the Incarnation.

John Main did not believe in forcing convictions on others but he did believe in breaking habits of thought which hold us back from full potential. He believed with deepening certainty that the Spirit is guiding the modern world through its crises by reawakening, in the midst of our confusion and anxiety, the memory of our destined holiness. The contemplative power of early Christianity, largely diverted to dogmatic and institutional structures, is now being released again. Not for a regression, but an advance into a universal, contemplative Christianity. The contemplative experience is simply pure attention to God in the present moment. And in the hearts of ordinary people this experience brings the Church, alive in prayer, to the centre of the world, as the heart of creation. As ordinary people go through the doors of their own being into the eternal now of God, the moment of Christ, the Church stirs as the Body of Christ in the here and now of Humanity.

John Main's teaching invites you to a way of prayer that by the virtue of its total simplicity, is universal. Anyone can meditate who wants to begin. Really to listen to what these pages are saying, over again in many different ways, is to hear a word that transcends the voice that carries it. We meditate to hear the Word itself with total attention and so to be united with it.

LAURENCE FREEMAN osb
Christian Meditation Centre
London
May 1988

The Art of Unlearning

At our community in Montreal I suggest to people that to try to come to terms with learning to meditate, they attend about ten weekly sessions of our Monday evening introductory group. When we approach most new experiences, we approach them carefully, because we have to learn something. But in meditation, the greater part of what we have to do is to unlearn. What we have to do is to surrender all the false images that we have of ourselves and of God. Meditation has always been understood, in the tradition, as an art. It is the art of all arts. And it is helpful to look at it like this, because it reminds us that we are undertaking the process of learning to be at one with our art. If you have ever seen a great violinist playing, the violinist and the violin become one in the exercise of the art; and as we look at it, it seems absolutely effortless. Whenever I myself have heard Isaac Stern or Yehudi Menuhin playing, in watching them I have been quite certain that I could do it just as well, it looks so easy. But of course the facility that the great artists have at being at one with their art comes from their practice, their daily practice. An artist of the eminence of Yehudi Menuhin even now practises for four hours every day.

Meditation and learning to meditate is a gradual process, and the most important element in it is the practice. We must meditate every day. As you know, to meditate is itself absolute simplicity. Sit down – the only essential rule of posture is that your spine is as upright (not stiff) as it can be – and sit still. To begin with you must really work hard at sitting still (just don't move!) and then close your eyes gently, and begin to say your word. The word I recommend to you is *maranatha*. Four equally-stressed syllables; ma ra na tha.

1

The Art of Unlearning

We cannot approach meditation hoping that we are going to be experts, proficient within a week or two (or within a year or two). What we require is the regular practice of meditating every morning and evening and a constant commitment to the practice. You can read all the books in the world about playing the flute, but until you pick up a flute and start to play, you will not really have begun. Once you understand that meditation is an art, you begin to understand that the practice of it is much more important than all the speculation about it. And so, we slowly come to understand that to learn to meditate we need discipline: the discipline of sitting down and sitting still and of saying our word, our mantra, from the beginning of our meditation until the end. This is a difficult thing to understand when you begin. We want to follow our thoughts, to come to new insights. Being religious people we may want to praise God, to say some prayer. But when you meditate you must transcend all thoughts and all words, and be silent, still and humble in the depths of your own being.

In meditation we learn to become progressively more simple, more humble, because the knowledge that we enter is progressively more unified. The art of meditation is the art of learning to say the mantra, learning to set it free in your heart, so that it sounds in your heart at all times as a focal point of stability within the depths of your being. The richness of the Christian vision of prayer, of meditation, of being, is that it is only in the depths of ourselves that we can encounter the mystery of God. The whole way of meditation is a way of non-violence and so the art of saying the mantra requires sustained delicacy and strength rather than force. These have to be sustained because we have to *learn* to say it. We have to learn, through thick and through thin, through difficult times and through good times, to abandon our own thoughts, plans and ideas as well as all our own images. And so, one of the things we must learn is to approach each meditation with a freshness of spirit. Each meditation is a new beginning, a fresh setting-out on the pilgrimage beyond self, beyond limitation into the wonder of God. What we seek to do when we meditate is *simply* to say our mantra as faithfully and as generously as we can.

The mystery of God is one of infinite generosity, a pouring out of infinite love, and we have to prepare our hearts to make them as generous and as loving as we can. So as we say our mantra, we let go of our thoughts, plans and problems in order to clear the way for God. This means that we must learn to say the mantra without expectations, without demands. In other words, we must become 'poor in spirit' and for most of us this is the greatest challenge. It will probably even be a quite unprecedented experience of a wholly selfless act: doing something with no concern whatever for what we are going to get out of it. When you are beginning it is very easy to say, 'Well, I'll try it. I'll meditate for six months and if it works out, I'll continue'. But if we want really to begin, we have to learn *from the beginning* to say the mantra unconditionally. It is a great act of faith. And naturally, in spite of all good intentions, we most of us start out with less than perfect attitudes. What, therefore, is of over-riding importance is that we remain as faithful as we can, as generous as we can, as undemanding as we can; and that we return daily to the practice. If you seriously want to learn to meditate, it is necessary to meditate for a minimum of twenty minutes each morning and each evening. The optimum time is about thirty minutes.

The wonder of this learning experience is that, as we continue to meditate, our motives are purified, by the experience itself, which is the experience of becoming more silent, more simple, more humble. But forget about the motives. The guarantee that we are on the path is that we continue to say the mantra from the beginning to the end. Saying the mantra is a marvellously simple, if demanding, way of committing ourselves to reality in its profoundest depths. The profoundest depths of which we are capable are the depths of our own spirit. And it is in these depths of our self, our spirit, that we encounter the Spirit of God. The extraordinary thing about the Christian proclamation is that every one of us is invited to enter profoundly into the depths of God's own Spirit. This is the teaching of St Paul writing to the Romans:

Now that we have been justified through faith, let us continue

3

at peace with God through our Lord Jesus Christ, through whom we have been allowed to enter the sphere of God's grace, where we now stand. (Rom. 5:1–2)

Meditation is the opening of our spirit to the truth that we have our being within the sphere of God's grace, 'where we now stand'.

A Way of Beginning

Our work as a community is to try to introduce people to the essence of Christian meditation. It flows from our conviction as monks that meditation is of supreme importance if a person is to understand the full wonder of the gift of his own being; and if he is going to understand, too, the full wonder of the gift of Christ each of us has received. But we have to start with ourselves. We have to start from where we are.

What I try to put before people is a way of starting on an inner pilgrimage that leads to knowledge, to wisdom, to love. The first thing to understand as we begin this process of pilgrimage is that it is extraordinarily simple. This itself is a big problem for us as men and women of the twentieth century. We are used to thinking of reality in terms of complexity. If, for example, you go to look for a new automobile the salesman will tell you of its fantastic complexity, such as the computer you set at the beginning of the journey which assesses your progress every fifty miles, with all sorts of permutations of information. The idea seems to be that complexity is one of the great selling points in the car. He does not tell you, of course, that in the first severe frost the computer will fail, so that when you try to find out your fuel consumption you start the radio instead. Complexity suggests sophistication to us, even when it leads to breakdown. What he means in trying to sell you the computer is that as it makes the car more complex, the vehicle is more worthy for you to own.

With such a consumerist conditioning, the difficulty of meditation for us is its sheer simplicity. Just learning, for example, to sit still sounds so obvious it seems to lack sophistication or cleverness. But be still we must, as we learn to bring body and mind to that point of integration and harmony that is the threshold of the spirit. That sounds so simple although it is not easy, that we dismiss it and look for something more complex to interest us. We must always bear in mind, in starting to meditate, that it is challengingly and absolutely simple. If that still means that it is not all that *easy*, it is because we are so used to complexity. If stillness is not easy it is because we are so used to distraction, constant movement and busyness.

Now let me try to describe how to come to the simplicity needed for prayer. When you prepare for meditation try to find a sitting posture that is both comfortable and alert. The only essential rule of posture is a straight back. Close your eyes and start repeating your mantra without moving either lips or tongue. And say the word continuously until the end of the meditation. It is difficult for Christians when they first hear about this to understand how it could even be prayer. How can this non-thinking state be significant in the life of a Christian? Is it just a way of relaxing? Has it really any ultimate significance in the Christian vision of life? If you persevere with meditation you will discover that significance for yourself.

The significance is that the gift of God in Jesus to each one of us is an absolute gift. Meditation is our absolute, accepting response. God has given us himself. Nothing has been kept back. He has given us the fullness of the divinity in the humanity of Jesus. A Christian life is our response to that gift and, just as the gift is absolute, so must our response be absolute and permanent. In responding to the gift of God in meditation we place ourselves wholly at his disposition. We do not even think any of our own thoughts. We do not even tell God of our own thoughts. We are simply and totally at his disposition by responding totally to the gift, body and mind, in absolute silence. The silence of meditation could be described as the *eternal* silence of God. So when people ask, 'How long will it take?' the answer is that it takes no time at all, or it takes the time of your morning meditation and your evening meditation. The gift is given. The Spirit is poured into the hearts of each one of us. All we have to do is to *realize* what is given to us by God in Jesus, through the Spirit. It is the task of our daily meditation to go beyond time in a way that transforms time by the gift of the Spirit. In your meditation at the beginning of each day you stand on the day's threshold holding the gift in open hands. You do not know what the day will bring. But you approach it in absolute faith and confidence because you approach it from the eternity of God. The beginning of every day is rooted in faith in God and in his goodness, his mercy, his compassion, and his love. That is how you start your day – not only thinking about these ideas but by entering into their reality in Jesus. That is the Christian vision: that Jesus lives in your hearts beyond ideas. The Spirit is poured into each of us in silence. And so that is the way you start the day, in faith, and by discovering that faith in the Spirit's silence of your own heart. When each day begins in this way, the goodness, compassion and love of Christ bless and fortify the work of the day with his active presence in our action and thoughts.

Again, when you come to your evening meditation, the whole of the day is gathered together. It is summed up in Jesus and in his presence in your heart. All the tensions, worries, as well as the joys, everything good and ill, is brought together in Jesus. But this is all dependent on practice. There is no way anyone can learn to meditate by reading books about meditation or by listening to talks on meditation. The only way we can learn is by meditating. That is why it is essential to meditate every day, each morning and evening. It is a considerable demand but one that leads us into the wonder of everything the gospel reveals. We discover in the experience of truly silent prayer what Jesus has achieved and what he has given to each one of us.

The secret of meditation is to be relaxed and alert, silent and simple. If you want to know why, then read St Paul writing to the Colossians where he speaks about the essence of the Christian message. This core-teaching is what meditation is about and in coming to understand the essence of Christianity in your own experience you find God in your own heart.

7

The secret is this: Christ in you, the hope of a glory to come. He it is whom we proclaim.

He rescued us from the domain of darkness and brought us away into the Kingdom of his dear Son in whom our release is secured and our sins forgiven. (Col. 1:27, 13–15)

The secret is not hidden: it is 'Christ in you'.

Straying from the Mantra

It is always very important to be clear about the basic way of meditating. Because it has to be clear, I think there is a real sense in which we cannot hear too often the way of meditating. And it is this: to learn to say your word, your mantra, from the beginning to the end of the meditation. That is something you have to relearn constantly because the temptation that most of us face is that our thoughts begin to take over. The thoughts are usually quite insidious because it can often be like 'I wonder would I be able to say my mantra better if I was sitting in the full lotus rather than the half lotus. Now, *how* could I learn to sit in the full lotus?' Ten minutes later you think of what you are going to have for dinner or do tomorrow, and so maybe twenty minutes later you get back to saying the mantra again. What you have to learn is that *the* important thing is to say the mantra from the beginning to the end, and when you find you have strayed from it, return to it immediately, not violently but gently, faithfully.

To learn to meditate we have to learn to be humble. We must know that we have something to learn and that we can only learn anything when we start to listen humbly. What does it mean to be humble? It means to begin to acknowledge that there is a reality outside of ourselves, that is greater than ourselves and that contains us. Humility is simply learning to find our place within that greater reality and we all have to learn to live in our place. The first thing to understand is that you *are* your own place. To come to terms with all reality, we must first come to terms with our own reality. It is in the stillness of meditation, the stillness of body and spirit which reveals the unity of body and spirit, that we enter the experience of knowing really that we *are*. We come to know this with absolute clarity and absolute certainty. Only then are we ready for the next step which is to go beyond ourselves, to rise beyond ourselves. The tragedy of the egoist is that the egoist does not know his or her place. The egoist thinks that he is at the centre of everything and sees everything, unreally, only in relation to himself.

Meditation and the constant return to it, every day of your life, is like cutting a pathway through to reality. Once we know our place, we begin to see everything in a new light because we have become who we really are. And becoming who we are, we can now see everything as it is and so begin to see everyone else as they are. The truest wonder of meditation is that we even begin to see God as God is. Meditation is therefore a way to stability. We learn through the practice and from the experience how to be rooted in our essential being. We learn that to be rooted in our essential being is to be rooted in God, the author and principle of all reality. And it is no small thing to enter reality, to become real, to become who we are, because in that experience we are freed from all the images that so constantly plague us. We do not have to be anyone's image of ourselves, but simply the real person we are.

Meditation is practised in solitude but it is the great way to learn to be in relationship. The reason for this paradox is that, having contacted our own reality, we have the existential confidence to go out to others, to meet them at their real level. and so the solitary element in meditation is mysteriously the true antidote to loneliness. Having contacted our conformity with reality, we are no longer threatened by the otherness of others. We are not always looking for an affirmation of ourselves. We are making love's search, looking for the reality of the other. In the experience of encountering the reality of the other, we discover our own existence enriched and deepened.

Meditation is demanding. We must learn to meditate whether we feel like it or not, whether it is raining or snowing, or the sun is shining and whatever is on television or whatever kind of day we have had. In the Christian vision of meditation, a perspective gained from the words of Jesus, we find the reality of the great paradox he teaches: if we want to find our lives we have to be prepared to lose them. In meditating, that is exactly what we do. We find ourselves because we are prepared to let go of ourselves, to launch ourselves out into the depths which soon appear to be the depths of God. The essential message of Christianity is that God is present in the depths of our human being. That is why we must learn humility. That is why we must learn silence; because we must enter those depths of our self to encounter the otherness of God and in that encounter, to discover our essential self in union with God.

Keep the elements of the practice clear. The practice itself is very simple. Find the quietest place, sit upright and sit still. The discipline of sitting still and not fidgeting is your first physical step into selflessnes. And then closing your eyes gently, say the mantra, say your word. *Maranatha*. Don't observe yourself, don't think about yourself, listen to the word as you recite it, silently, interiorly in your heart. Continue *saying* the word, *reciting* the word, *listening* to the word for the entire time of your meditation. When you begin you must begin in faith. Do not give up too easily, but if you do give up, start again. Sometimes it takes us a half a dozen false starts before we begin the journey of our life that takes us into life.

Reflect on these words from the first Letter of St John in relation to your life's journey:

> Our theme is the word of life. This life was made visible; we have seen it and bear our testimony; we here declare to you the eternal life which dwelt with the Father and was made visible to us. What we have seen and heard we declare to you, so that you and we together may share in a common life, that life we share with the Father and his Son Jesus Christ. . . Here is the message we heard from him, and pass on to you: God is light and in him there is no darkness at all. (1 Jn. 1:1–5)

It is our call as Christians to come into that light and so to leave utterly behind all darkness. The way to that light is the way of humility in silence; the way of the mantra.

11

Tension and Attention

The nature of prayer is undivided attention and meditation is a way to total alertness and pure attentiveness of spirit. When we think of being alert, we tend to think of it as a difficult state of consciousness to reach and even more difficult to maintain for long, because we associate it with the state of tension. It seems like staying awake when we would rather just relax or go to sleep. We can escape this confusion, which so blurs our understanding of prayer, if we distinguish between tension and attention. Prayer is a-ttention, a state of non-tension. It is true though that a certain degree of effort is required to move into this state of consciousness. But it is the same effort that is required to persevere in meditation. The only effort is the effort of perseverance. Once we have made the commitment that we will meditate, then paradox becomes the rule that illuminates everything in meditation. The effort becomes effortless and instead of tension, we know peace.

The state of alertness that we are then in is not so much tense as full of a peace, a deep order, that bestows true tranquillity. The only tension required is the tension required for anything that is in a state of expansion; the order contains its own tension. We need only remember that it is this state of peacefulness that we were created for. A state of alert, wakeful peacefulness and openness, it is the most natural state for any of us to be in. Its naturalness explains why we are so restless and discontented until we have found our way into this state of consciousness. We tend to imagine that this state of readiness is merely one of waiting, when we are saying the mantra until . . . what? We are just waiting and we don't like the idea of waiting indefinitely. In fact, we like things to arrive at our

12

bidding. To have to wait seems to us to involve a certain humiliation, like joining the end of a long queue. But waiting is only a metaphor to describe this state of consciousness, a metaphor drawn from the world of time and then applied to something which is timeless. What we are waiting for has in fact already reached us. It has already been achieved and Jesus has achieved this state of realization. He is alert, attentive, peaceful. He is at prayer. He has done so in time, but for all eternity. So when we meditate and wait upon the Lord we are not waiting for something to happen. We are simply waiting for something that is happening to be realized. And when it *is* realized we will not say, 'Ah, at last it's come'. Rather we will say, 'Now I recognize what I know has always been'. The state of consciousness that Jesus talks about – wakefulness, alertness – is a state of realization and when we are meditating we are becoming realized. In essence it is a process of opening rather than of concentration.

The tension we need to remain attentive is expansive rather than restrictive. Unrestrictive tension is another paradox of the pilgrimage. Our difficulty in living with paradox explains why we can so easily lose heart in the face of the challenge to persevere, because we can see only the tension and so fail to understand what a unique kind of tension it is. It is the tension of expansion. It is the tension of the springboard, the energy that continually launches us more profoundly into the depths. Nearly all the terms we use to describe the experience of prayer contain images of energy and the nature of energy is that it cannot be seen in itself but only in its manifestation. This discrete presence is the mystery of the Spirit which is the energy of God, the expansiveness of God. The Spirit is the creative tension between the Father and the Son and we can only know this energy of the Spirit once it has entered us. It cannot be known merely objectively, merely analytically. When it has entered us it has already begun to transform us into its own nature, into the pure energy of love; and our times of meditation are times when this energy is allowed absolute sway, absolute freedom in our being. So it follows that when we meditate with an open, pure and attentive heart we rise from our meditation renewed, energized, vitalized and refreshingly humbled as well.

Our humility arises from the fact that we are naturally happy that we are being transformed. We are no longer trying to hang on to our own identity, which would be the way to remain forever anonymous. Only when we are fully and undividedly attentive to the energy of God and therefore totally lost to ourselves, can we be transformed into the person we are called to be, the person we essentially are. Here we come to the heart of the mystery.

We encounter this transforming power, the love which reveals to us true identity through union, in the human consciousness of Christ. The wonder of the Christian revelation is that the consciousness of Christ dwells in our hearts and once we accept that, then the most important task of our life becomes to be fully open to it. Our attentiveness to God, our prayer, is eternally united to the indwelling consciousness of Christ at prayer within us. Here is the starting-point for our discovery of God, as St Paul immortally expressed it in words of revelation, words that sprang from the deepest experience:

For the Spirit explores everything, even the depths of God's own nature. Among men who knows what a man is but the man's own spirit within him? In the same way, the Spirit of God knows what God is. This is the spirit that we have received from God, and not the spirit of the world, so that we may know all that God of his own grace has given us; and, because we are interpreting spiritual truths to those who have the Spirit, we speak of these gifts of God in words found for us not by our human wisdom but by the Spirit. A man who is unspiritual refuses what belongs to the Spirit of God, it is folly to him; he cannot grasp it, because it needs to be judged in the light of the Spirit. But a man gifted with the Spirit can judge the worth of everything, but is not himself subject to judgement by his fellow-men. For (in the words of Scripture) 'who knows the mind of the Lord? Who can advise him?' (1 Cor. 2:11–16)

St Paul ends this paragraph with perhaps the most astonishing words in the Scriptures, 'We however possess the mind of Christ'. This is simply what our meditation is about; being open – wholly, attentively and wakefully – to this great gift we are given, the human consciousness of Christ alive in our heart.

Essentially Free

Meditation is rightly seen as the way of spiritual growth, of human development. But it is above all else a gentle process of growing into the freedom that is beyond all limitations. Once we pass a limitation that has previously held us back, we discover that we are free from it for all eternity. Time is so precious because we must use the opportunity it gives us to grow as completely as we can beyond all limitations so that we can enter into eternity, eternal life, as persons who are essentially free. This process of growth into freedom is an essential aspect of the divine dimension. God is the one who is infinite growth, infinite and perfect freedom. God is the one who is complete. As I have suggested to you before, divine perfection is not a static achievement. To be complete is simply to be free of all the limitations that would restrict us from infinite expansion. That is why the state of completeness is always present, never future, never past. For God is always NOW.

Our meditation is always concerned with another step deeper into the present moment, another step into the eternal now of God. Every time we meditate, we take a step further into the divine life, wholly present and yet wholly expansive and expanding. Like all growth, this involves pain. It is the pain of maturing, of ripening and it means leaving earlier stages of development behind. Part of the difficulty is that we have to learn to leave behind not just part of ourselves but the whole of ourselves that was the past. We can only become fully present to the now of this moment if we can leave the past behind. What we try to do instead is to maintain observation points, base camps, along every stage of our growth. At each of these observation points we are loath to let go of any part of ourselves in favour of the new stage of growth. It becomes simpler, and even easier, if we recognize that it is not part of ourselves we need be concerned about leaving, but our whole self. If we refuse this, opting instead for piecemeal surrenders, then instead of life being an experience of growth we find our lives contracting.

At each stage of growth we have to leave all of ourselves behind in order to go forward, becoming an ever new creation. This is precisely what we do every time we meditate. Each occasion we sit down to meditate, everything we have done until that moment, including everything we have been until that moment, is simply abandoned. The more fully the past is abandoned, the more fully renewed we are as we return to our present day. So meditation is a continuous breakthrough into the present moment, into the present moment of God. The breakthrough is not restricted to isolated experiences and that is why concern for what one is experiencing from day to day is so counter-productive to real spiritual growth and development. Such a concern tries to fix God in time and therefore to stifle God's own free expansion of spirit. As soon as we do this we experience not God but only our own egotistical image of God.

Strictly speaking, meditation does not give us any experience of God. God does not 'experience' himself but rather he *knows*. For him to experience himself would suggest a divided consciousness. What meditation does is to take us into the life of God, the life full of knowledge of the Word begotten from self-transcendence. This is why meditation is an entry into divinization through Jesus. Through him we become one with God. With him we utterly transcend ourselves, leaving the whole of ourselves behind and becoming a new creation in him. In him, meditation is itself the process of self-transcendence. To the degree that we are transcending ourselves we are sharers in the divine nature because we are learning to be one with the power of love. Our growth in meditation cannot be seen in the accumulation of experiences but rather in the transcending of all experience. What we so often call an experience is only a memory. But in the eternal act of creation which is the life of

17

the trinitarian God everything is present. Each of us by our own little self-transcendence is nevertheless empowered to become one with God. This is what we must never forget.

Each time we sit down to meditate we enter into that oneness, the oneness of God who is now, the oneness of God who is love. We cannot adequately conceptualize all this. It is too simple for our mind to comprehend. But what we can do is to sit down and say our mantra with humility, with fidelity and with absolute trust in the goodness of God who calls us beyond our every limitation. He calls us, such is the marvel of the Christian revelation, to expand into infinity with him. The more we do contemplate the wonder of our vocation the more humble we must become, the more poor in spirit. We become humble, we become poor in spirit, by our fidelity to our mantra. As we progress we have to become *more* faithful.

It sometimes seems at the beginning that as we make progress we will not have to say the mantra with quite the same fidelity in the future. But, as we do actually progress, we discover that we must enter more deeply into that poverty, that humility and that fidelity to which it is the grace of the mantra to lead us. A deepening commitment to the mantra sharpens our wonder at the purpose of our pilgrimage, which St Paul described as 'being manifested with Christ'.

> Did you not die with Christ and pass beyond reach of the elemental spirits of the universe? Then why behave as though you were still living the life of the world? Why let people dictate to you? . . . Were you not raised to life with Christ? Then aspire to the realm above, where Christ is, seated at the right hand of God, and let your thoughts dwell on that higher realm, not on this earthly life. I repeat, you died; and now your life lies hidden with Christ in God. When Christ, who is our life, is manifested, then you too will be manifested with him in glory. (Col. 2:20, 3:1–4)

What Jesus has Done

It is the great good fortune of monks to be able to stand aside from much of the hurly burly, with time to reflect and to consider the basic processes of the human condition. It is our guiding conviction that the life and teaching, the death and resurrection of Jesus have radically transformed the potential for the development of human consciousness. It is our conviction, too, that if we want to live our lives fully, then we need, somehow or other, to come to terms with this fact of the life and death and resurrection of Jesus, because what he has done and what he now is have placed new realms of experience within our reach. No longer are we cut off from the full experience of God. We are invited to enter right into the heart of the divine mystery and every one of us is invited. Above all, it is our working conviction as monks that there is nothing to be gained merely by talking about all this. To talk about the transformation of consciousness arising from the life of Jesus will get us nowhere unless we actually take the practical steps to enter into the process of transformation he initiates. The one thing we have to share with everyone is that it is the *practice* of meditation that is of supreme importance.

There is a real danger in being able to theorize eloquently about God and godliness, when such theorizing is based only on more theory and never on experience. But the theory, the theology, is of real value and we need to be clear about it. What Jesus has done for us, in the language of the New Testament, is to send his Spirit to dwell in our hearts. His Spirit is open in love to God the Father and by our being open, in love, to the Spirit of Jesus, we also are transported into the love of the Father, with him and through him. In other words human consciousness, and that means the personal consciousness of every human individual, is summoned to an infinite expansion, infinite development. The essential meaning of the whole human process is that we are summoned to full maturity and we can only come to ultimate maturity by meeting and responding to the consciousness of Jesus. What Jesus has done, what he has achieved in his life, in effect, is to bring the divine within the ambiance of every man and woman alive. The question however remains: how do we open our human consciousness to the human consciousness of Jesus? It is here that we turn from theory to meditation.

In meditation we seek to disassemble the barriers that we have set up around ourselves and that cut us off from the consciousness of the presence of Jesus within our own heart. In meditating we start the process of dismantling the ego and its persistent attempt to place ourselves at the centre. We begin to understand that God is at the centre and so our whole perspective and orientation changes. In the practice of meditation, we begin to learn what real humility is about; being ourself in our proper place. Meditation also teaches us that we can reach God the Father, *through* the human consciousness of Jesus, the Son, because we discover by meditating in faith that Jesus is the bridge that takes us to the further shore. He is the ferry that takes us across the little tributary of egoism and launches us into the mainstream of divine love. Egoism flows into backwaters of isolation. Meditation leads us through this isolation into the oceanic love of God.

Gradually we come to realise that love is the basis of all reality and that we are invited to live fully in this love through our commitment to gentleness, to compassion, to understanding. The great fact of the experience of meditating is that once we do enter into the human consciousness of Jesus we begin to see as he sees, to love as he loves, to understand as he understands and to forgive as he forgives. Our angle of vision on the whole of creation is profoundly altered. Once expanded it need never again contract, and will not, if we always remember the pre-eminence of the practice.

It is, practically, necessary to meditate every day, morning and evening. It is necessary in order to ground and root our lives in the foundational reality of Christ's living Spirit that is manifested in every aspect of human life. But it is especially characterized by its gentleness and the powerful gift of forgiveness. You may well ask, 'How will sitting to meditate bring *me* to this compassion and forgiveness; how will the mantra lead me to this love?' When you begin you have to take that on faith. There is no way of answering that question except for yourself, through the practice.

Basically, though, the reason is this; what stops us from knowing and showing compassion, what stops us from recognizing and entering the presence of Jesus in our heart as the presence of the pure Spirit of Love, is our own egoism. What that means, is that we cannot be open to this innermost dimension of reality because we are thinking about our surface selves; we are locked into our self. Saying the mantra is like unlocking the door of our heart. The mantra is like the key unlocking the door to allow the pure light of love to flood in. Although powerful, it is a gentle process. Do not expect dramatic miracles. In fact do not expect anything. Be humbly content every morning and evening, to return simply to the practice. In the practice itself you will find the powers of gentleness, forgiveness and compassion, all revealing themselves. Do not fear their power to change you.

When you begin you may have many questions about the technique, the technical aspects of meditating. How should you say your mantra? Should you, for example, say it to your breathing? Or should you say it to your heartbeat? My recommendation is, when you begin, begin as simply as you possibly can. Just say it. If it is natural for you to say it to your heartbeat, say it to your heartbeat. If it is natural for you to say it to your breathing, say it to your breathing. If it does not seem that you say it to either, say it as you can. The technical questions are secondary and many will be answered naturally through the experience gained by the practice itself.

Two sayings of Jesus are of great importance when we are beginning to meditate. The first is, 'Unless you become like a little child, you cannot enter the Kingdom of heaven'. To learn to meditate we have to learn to be very simple. We have to re-learn how to be childlike. We have to learn, as a child learns, by accepting the teaching on faith and by devoting ourselves to its practice. We have to learn to rediscover the capacity for wonder which comes with faith and practice combined. We so easily lose that as we lose our early simplicity. Meditating is a returning to innocence and a sign of it is a returning to a state of wonder.

The second helpful phrase of Jesus is, 'No one can be a follower of mine unless he leaves self behind'. In saying your mantra you have to let go of your own thoughts, your own theories and ideas, your imagination, fears and daydreams, and simply be there, listening to the sound of the mantra. Whatever you do, do not think about yourself. If you find, as all of us do, that it is difficult to sustain this, as soon as you discover that you are distracted, or that you are again thinking about yourself, return very gently and very humbly to the mantra. The mantra is a great teacher of humility. As we all discover when we begin to meditate it is difficult for us to stay even for a couple of moments, silently and faithfully in the presence of the Lord.

The practice of meditation is an acceptance of the primacy of the revelation that the Lord's presence is real and personal. We have so largely lost the early Christian sense of urgency and wonder at what Jesus has accomplished.

> All I care for is to know Christ, to experience the power of his resurrection, and to share his sufferings, in growing conformity with his death, if only I may finally arrive at the resurrection from the dead. (Phil. 3:10–11)

Experience the power of his resurrection. The power of the resurrection of Jesus is the power of unlimited life, eternal life. It is what each of us is invited to experience now, in this life. '*All* I care for is to experience the power of his resurrection.'

The Unreality of Fear

The basis of our Christian faith is that God is supreme reality. God is the one who is wholly real, the one who is. Nothing exists or can exist outside the divine reality. If we think that anything can exist outside of God, we are living and dealing with illusion and fantasy. The traditional Christian understanding of sin depends upon this very insight, because we are under the power of 'sin' when we live in the belief that anything can exist outside of God. This power controls us when we try, for example, to act as though we are acting outside of God or to love as though we were loving outside of God. Everything, therefore, that we call sin, we might equally well call illusion because of its unreality, its departure from the order of reality. Sin is evil precisely because it is in opposition to the structure of reality, the structure of being, the structure of love. All sin is illusion masquerading as reality.

In the Christian vision our redemption from sin is liberation from illusion by the terrible reality of the cross. By ourselves we could never have freed ourselves from the power of illusion and fantasy. And, as we all know from bitter experience, illusion does have a sort of magnetic hold over us. Fantasy does often have some kind of negative, infernal momentum. The longer we stay enthralled by illusion, the stronger its hold upon us. The only power that can free us from this destructive fascination with unreality, with illusion, with sin, is the power of reality itself. If we look at Calvary and can see its terrible reality, we know what we mean when we say that we are redeemed by the unconditional love of God. We know, too, that it is only God's love, this infinite source of power, that can smash the power of the father of lies. Satan's title is well chosen, the one who engenders falsehood and deals in illusion.

Now as Christian thinkers or apologists we speak of God as supreme reality, but as ordinary Christian human beings with hearts of flesh, we say and know that God is Love. This is to say the same thing but from a deeper, more integrated and fully conscious perception. We experience reality because we are capable of loving and of being loved. To know love and to be known in love is to know reality, and the experience of knowing reality is the experience of being freed from the isolation of illusion. In the experience of being touched by another, of allowing ourselves to be touched and then entering into the wonder of the response that love evokes, we are launched into reality. Listen to St John writing on this:

> The man who does not love is still in the realm of death, for everyone who hates his brother is a murderer, and no murderer, as you know, has eternal life dwelling within him. It is by this that we know what love is: that Christ laid down his life for us. And we in our turn are bound to lay down our lives for our brothers. (1 Jn 3:15–16)

And then listen to how he goes on:

> My children, love must not be a matter of words or talk; it must be genuine, and show itself in action. (1 Jn 3:18)

The difference between our state of mind when we are in love, compared with our attitude when we are in a state of fear or isolation, is something we all know. Love evokes a spirit of joy in life; it evokes its variety, its unexpectedness, its colour. And the more generously we allow this spirit of love to expand within us, the more we become other-centred; the more we find our perfection in the other, our fulfilment in the other. It is in this experience that we let go of self-consciousness and discover our real consciousness. We discover it in contact with another real consciousness. Out of this encounter comes the creative energy that enables us to work selflessly, lovingly.

As we read the gospel we see that a choice is set before us. The alternative is between love and fear. Fear is destructive and corrosive, whether it is the fear of plague, war or famine or whether it is fear of supernatural, angry, vengeful gods who must be placated by compulsive rituals. The difference between a barbaric world and a civilized world is that barbarism thrives on fear. Civilization thrives on a love that gives birth to vigour, energy, vitality, creativity. Barbaric energy is negative; its main thrust is destructive and its principal art is war. The principal art of the Christian life is peace. Our commitment to meditation is our openness to the peace of God's redemptive love, our total acceptance of it, our abandonment of self-fixation and our commitment to self-giving. While we are saying our mantra we cannot be thinking about ourselves, and it is precisely self-obsession that leads us back into fantasy. So when we find that we have stopped saying the mantra, that our mind is drifting, we must simply return to it and, with it, to reality. We return, that is, to God present in our hearts. Or in other words, we return to a faith that propels us beyond ourselves into God. We all know that this self-transcendence is our salvation. Fundamentally, we all know that we must go to meet it in the silence of our hearts. The alternatives are reality or illusion.

The root-function of fantasy is that it attempts to turn us from the fears and anxieties we feel by creating an alternative reality. But what happens is that the fear is just buried deeper and deeper in our hearts. The root-function of the gospel, which is really the only root, is to expel fear, to pluck it out by the roots so that we can then go deeper and deeper into a fearless heart and encounter profoundest love. The great gift we have to share with the world is our experience of reality. Listen to St John again:

Dear friends, let us love one another, because love is from God. Everyone who loves is a child of God and knows God, but the unloving know nothing of God. For God is love; and his love was disclosed to us in this, that he sent his only Son into the world to bring us life. The love I speak of is not our love for God, but the love he showed to us in sending his Son as the remedy for the defilement of our sins. If God thus loved us, dear friends, we in turn are bound to love one another . . . his love is brought to perfection within us. Here is the proof that we dwell in him and he dwells in us: he has imparted his spirit to us. (1 Jn 4:7–13)

Surface and Depth

One of the great truths that appears in the traditional wisdom in almost every variety of that tradition, is that we have to discover our own inner reality. The problem for us all is to avoid living our lives on the basis of other people's experience, not to live our lives, in other words, second hand. And to do this we have to go beyond the surface of things. We cannot live our lives by always encountering reality on a two-dimensional level. The Tao Te Ching expresses it like this: *The truly great man dwells on what is real and not on what is on the surface.* What is real is the inner structure, the inner reality. It is, I think, a general law of the human condition that in order to understand the universe we must understand ourselves. In order to value the cosmos, we have to learn to value ourselves. It is only when we understand and value ourselves that we can transcend ourselves, rise above ourselves; in the words of Jesus, 'leave ourselves behind'.

The journey of meditation is the journey to depth, which is a depth both of understanding and of being. It is not a journey, in the first instance, that is made by analysis, or reflection. We must first have something real and firsthand to analyse or reflect on. The journey of meditation primarily invites us to silence, to stillness and to reverence in the depths of our being. Part of our problem in responding to the invitation is that we are always analysing the surface and hoping to come to depth of understanding as a result of surface judgement. Our understanding is usually merely reflections off the surface. But we can only understand the surface if we journey into the depths. What the journey primarily requires of us is simplicity. It also requires of us, faith and ongoing faithfulness. Meditation is the simple faith process whereby we enter our inner reality. The extraordinary thing about this process is that in entering our inner being we make contact with the essential structure of all being, of all reality. We are all careless about using words like God, truth, being and reality because so often they are not words that spring directly from within ourselves. A good part of the anxiety that so many people feel, arises from the fact that for much of our lives we have only a second-hand grasp of reality. Too often we only contact it through words.

The process of meditation demands simplicity. Each of us has to learn simply to let go, to launch out into the depths. Yet all of us have a certain fear of that, particularly when we suspect that the depths are infinite. That is in fact what the journey is about, launching out into the infinite depths of God. Think about the process for a moment. When you meditate, try to sit as still as possible. By stillness of body you physically anchor your being in its place and you stay rooted in that place in a deepening stillness, which leads to silence and to reverence. Then as you close your eyes gently, begin to recite in your heart, interiorly, silently, your word, your mantra: *maranatha*. Meditation is a process of absolute gentleness. You do not recite your word with violence. It is not like a hammer on an anvil. We must learn to recite our word with delicacy and with gentleness. And we must recite it throughout the meditation, from the beginning to the end, listening to it, not thinking about ourselves, not thinking about God, not thinking about the meaning of the mantra. But just, in absolute simplicity, reciting it continuously. The mantra anchors us in depth of being.

When anyone begins he or she has to take it on faith that the recitation of the word is a significant activity. You have to take it on faith that the journey of meditation is into depth of understanding, depth of experience, which leads to an utterly personal conviction about the reality in which we are rooted. We make our act of faith on the authority of a tradition in which men and women have trodden this path throughout the ages and have done so with generosity, with love and fidelity and, in the process, have been brought to understanding, to compassion, to wisdom.

The call to meditate is an invitation to stop leading our lives on the basis of second-hand evidence. It is a call to each one of us to come to grips with our spiritual capacity and so to discover for ourselves the astonishing richness of the human capacity that is anchored in the divine reality, in the divine life-power. And it is also an invitation to be simply open to that power, to be energized by it and to be swept along by it, into the depths of the divine reality itself.

The lived process is very important. We must always beware of being intoxicated merely by the message, merely by the good news, merely by the ideas of the gospel. We must enter in, taste and see. And meditation is the process of entering in, of tasting, of seeing. Saying your mantra every day, making the time available for meditation, morning and evening, and placing your spiritual journey and the spiritual reality at the centre of your life, *that* is what is important.

This is a traditional wisdom shared by the Sufi poet, Attar. In these lines he describes so aptly what the journey of meditation is about, why it is so important that each of us comes in to full contact with our own spiritual capacity.

Come, you lost atoms to your centre draw near and be the eternal mirror that you saw.

Rays that have wandered into darkness wide, back unto your sun, subside.

That is what meditation is about – returning to your centre and finding that your centre is the gateway to the centre of All. And for that we have to stop living on the surface, we have to come to the depths. Jesus described it in these words:

Think of the lilies: they neither spin nor weave; yet I tell you, even Solomon in all his splendour was not attired like one of these. But if that is how God clothes the grass, which is growing in the field today, and tomorrow is thrown on the stove, how much more will he clothe you! How little faith you have! And so you are not to set your mind on food and drink; you are not to worry. For all these are things for the heathen to run after; but you have a Father who knows that you need them. No, you must set your mind upon his kingdom, and all the rest will come to you as well. (Lk 12:27–31)

That is what meditation is: setting our mind on the kingdom, on the power of God, on the divine reality.

The Mantra and Boredom

Modern advertizing often presents as the most attractive feature of its products, the fact that they are new. With familiar products also you are promised the *new*, improved formula. One of the results is that we tend to be searching for novelty as a criterion of value. And yet, in our experience, we often find only dull routine. One of the great problems of modern life is that so many people, for large parts of their life, experience a terrible and deadening boredom.

For many people the first glance at meditation makes it seem to them that it, too, will soon become another exercise in dull repetition. This summer I was giving a retreat in a convent in Ireland and one of the nuns there, having heard a talk on meditation and the mantra, came to me and said, 'Oh Father, I could never do that. No, no, I could never do it. It would be awful'. Her understanding of the mantra was that it would be totally trivial for her because of its dull repetitiveness. I hope she did begin to meditate, though, despite her fears, because only a little experience of really *learning* to say the mantra (and this is the art of meditation) would have changed her mind – to understand that the art of meditation is simply *setting the mantra free* within your heart. The difficulty of this for us is that we always want to be in control. It is very difficult for us as westerners to learn to set the mantra free, to let it sound, to let it sing in our heart in a sort of glorious liberty.

One of the biggest religious problems that we face is really allowing God to be free. So often we want to control him, getting him to see everything from our point of view and to make things turn out as we would want them to. But setting the mantra free in your heart is a preparation, indeed a sacrament, for allowing God to be totally free in your heart, at the centre of your life. Freedom can be frightening, challenging, frustrating. But it is never boring. The right kind of repetition is necessary to set us free but freedom as exercised is never repetitious. To be free ourselves we have to learn to set God free, free to lead us and to love us. As we all know from our human relationships, there can be no love without freedom. Once we love we enter into the greatest tyranny there is because we become wholly at the disposition of the other. That is exactly the experience of Christian prayer, of Christian meditation: to be wholly at the disposition of God.

Saying the mantra can never be mere repetition. Each time we say it we ratify our personal entry into the reality of God in whom all things are made new. Ritual itself – all true ritual – is making the eternal reality present in time. And ritual is at the other extreme from dull repetition. Repetition is merely a closed routine, but in ritual we enter into the totality of the expansive mystery of being. It is total because it combines the mystery of our own being with the mystery of the being of God. Each time we say the mantra we find our way more deeply into the presentness of God, the one who is and who describes himself as 'I Am'. Daily meditation is a ritual loss of self but it is also much more than a loss of self. It is an entering into ultimate being, ultimate reality, ultimate love. This is made possible as we become detached from our own limited way of seeing and feeling and understanding; as we open our hearts to the totality of perception and consciousness. In meditation and through the silence that the mantra leads us to, we come to that greatest human experience: we know ourselves to be 'known'. We understand that we are understood and, in the experience of coming into the presence of love, we discover that we are lovable.

How long does it take? It does not matter how long it takes. All that matters is that we are under way. All that matters is that we learn to let go, deeply enough, totally enough and sincerely enough, to be able to say our mantra with total attention and total generosity. To meditate all that is required is that total generosity which is a human generosity born of faith.

It is our faith in the reality of God, which is so difficult for modern men and women. It is also faith in the reality of ourselves, which is perhaps even more difficult for us as modern people with our conditioned self-doubt and complex systems of dependency. But in saying the mantra, in meditating every morning and every evening, we discover faith and we discover it very close to us in the person of Jesus. Through our relationship with him we can go where it would otherwise be closed to us to go.

So now, my friends, the blood of Jesus makes us free to enter boldly into the sanctuary by the new, living way which he has opened for us through the curtain, the way of his flesh. (Heb. 10:19–20)

People often say to me, 'Isn't this way of meditation a way of ignoring the humanity of Christ?' If only we can learn to say our mantra we will discover the fullness of that humanity, the fullness of Christ's love, close to us, present to us, in our hearts.

Liberty demands Detachment

As with anything we can turn our thought to, there are positive and negative aspects of meditation. If you think of the positive side of the coin, what meditation is about is a wonder-filled openness to all that is – to essential and basic reality. And the fruit of meditation is simply the courage to be, to be who you are and to live your life with all the fullness of the life-force which is given to you. It is to be in relationship with others because you come into contact with your own existence as relationship. And so to meditate is simply to set out on this path that leads to full wakefulness and the fullness of a loving life. But you must also look at the other side, the negative aspect. Our society is much more attracted to words like 'life-force', 'positive thinking', 'fullness', 'satisfaction' or 'fulfil-ment'. We can forget, though, that to set out on this path means that we must not only positively choose but also that we must positively reject.

Detachment is a concept of supreme importance in every school of meditation. Yet detachment is a word that is so little understood in our modern world that we are frightened of the concept. You have only to reflect for a few clear moments, however, to see that to be in a state of fulfilment we must enjoy full liberty: we cannot be in *any* sort of bondage. In other words, we must be detached from everything that hinders absolute freedom whether the attachment is passive or nega-tive; whether it concerns physical, mental or spiritual levels; whether the unfreedom is our own fault or has an inherited or conditioned cause. The invitation that each one of us is given is to come to that liberty of spirit which is total. It is obvious that there is no way of coming to that without detachment. But it is harder for us to see the force of Francis Thompson's words, 'All things betray thee who betrayest Me'. We ourselves betray the Master and Truth when we allow anything to cloud our vision of the one who is. The call to fullness of life is the call to purity of heart, to clarity of vision. Detachment is simply the way of keeping that clarity crystal clear. To be detached from our possessions, for example, is to be free from our possessions – to possess them, if necessary, yet not be possessed *by* them. In many ways it is easier to be detached from our material possessions than from the less solid objects we cling to. In meditation we learn to be detached from our thoughts, our pleasant and unpleasant feelings, our desires, even from our self-consciousness. This not only seems to our modern minds to be an impossibility, but it even seems to be a scandal that anybody should seriously propose this. But this is exactly the truth. It is the truth proclaimed by Jesus and the truth lived by the saints and sages down through the ages.

Consider the saying of Jesus that whoever cares for his own safety is lost but whoever will let himself be lost 'for my sake' will find his true self. To meditate is to lose yourself, to become absorbed in God, to be utterly lost in the generous immensity that we call God. None of us can ever find our true selves, we can never come into contact with full meaning or enter full understanding unless we are prepared for this way of letting ourselves be lost for the sake of the kingdom. None of us, in other words, can come to knowledge without faith. Fullness of knowledge is impossible without fullness of faith. And meditation is the way of faith because it is an entry into the otherness of God, and to enter on this way, to tread this path with true sincerity, we must learn to take the attention wholly off ourselves and to look only ahead. We must learn to look into pure love. The way to learn is the way of the mantra.

When you meditate day by day just say your mantra, sound it in your heart. Do not ask yourself, 'What am I getting out of this?' 'Am I enjoying this?' 'What insights am I getting?' 'How am I feeling?' All those questions can only lead us further down the blind alley of the ego. Recite your mantra and nothing else. The only problem of meditating is the simplicity of it. If only we could learn the simplicity to say our word like a child, with childlike faith, we would lose ourselves. We would lose ourselves in God and in losing ourselves we would find our way into relationship with all. We would find our way into love.

The Supreme Value

It is said that you can never convince anyone by argument. Nor can we convince ourselves of the truth of any statement by ideas alone. There is always another argument, always qualifying ideas. Spiritual truths are equally difficult to communicate by words because of the part paradox plays in them. In fact paradox is the way to avoid the mistake of linking the truth to the ideas or words alone.

Take the statement that we need to renounce ourselves in order to follow the spiritual path. This is a truth, but one that is contained also in the statement that we need to find ourselves if we are to find God. Between these two poles, of self-renunciation and self-discovery, we find the mid-point of the purely simple statement, that in prayer we are simply being ourselves. Let us start from this point.

Learning to meditate is learning to become a really harmonious person. There is nothing life-denying or self-rejecting about meditation. It is simply the way to get every aspect of our life into a harmonious relationship with every other aspect. If we were to try to achieve this by thought alone we would be defeated by the enormous complexity of it, but prayer is deeper and more powerful than thought. Our intellect and our emotions need not compete with one another and prayer harmonizes them so that they work together in peaceful complementarity. Every time we sit down to meditate we enter into a state of oneness where the whole of our life gently shakes together in the presence of God. God is one and he calls us to be one. There is a real point therefore in the *Cloud of Unknowing* calling meditation the process of one-ing, becoming one. By analysis it is possible to discover and endlessly to uncover all the disparate elements in our life and personal history, but in meditation we tread a path of synthesis whereby all the various, happy and unhappy, elements are bound together in the knowledge that we are one with God. It is a discovery that each of us is invited to make personally. Each one of us accepts a personal responsiblity for meditating, for sitting down, morning and evening, and for saying our mantra. Accepting and fulfilling this responsibility is a powerful factor in our developing into full personhood.

It might seem to you as you read these encouragements to meditate or as you attend a weekly group, or simply meditate every day, that you know all this and have nothing more to learn. There is a real sense in which you do know it and a real sense in which you have nothing more to learn. If you can fully learn and absorb that truth, you have learnt everything! The dynamic of learning it is that, in saying our mantra, in the daily return to the discipline, we gradually find out how to look beyond ourselves. We learn to see with a vision that focuses ahead of us, in God. In that focusing of everything in God (everything that we are), everything in our life becomes aligned on God and is rightly set into its proper place. Meditating is powerful because it leads us into this right order, into this tranquillity and peace.

Our order of values is gradually changed. Instead of our value system being based on the ego, on personal success or self-promotion, self-preservation or similar limiting factors, our value system becomes based on God. A revelation then takes place in our own hearts through this inner conversion, as we discover the presence of Jesus there. We discover his revelation that God is love. And this brings us to the conclusion that unleashes great power – that there is only one thing that matters ultimately and it is the personal and social value of supreme importance – which is that we grow in love. Everything else is secondary. Everything else is consequential. Once this insight becomes powerful enough, our lives are irreversibly transformed, because we then see the greater reality of other-centred values such as compassion, tolerance, forgiveness, and justice. We begin, therefore, to become truly spiritual people.

We are then in touch with life at its centre; and remember, God is the centre, God is love and Jesus is the revelation of his love.

This is not just some beautiful theory. It is the most practical consequence of the very practical practice of meditating every day of our lives, every morning and every evening. For that half an hour every morning and every evening we are focused beyond ourselves. Through the working of the Holy Spirit our spirit is expanding, our heart is enlarging, we are becoming more generous. The change in us comes about because, in meditation, we encounter and embrace the power that makes this change possible. All of us would presumably like to be more kind, more understanding, more selfless, more sympathetic, more compassionate and so on. But, at the same time, we recognize ourselves as weak, mortal, fallible human beings. This recognition often induces us to protect our vulnerability. What we discover in meditation is the power source that enables us to live without the anxiety of having to protect ourselves; it is established right at the centre of our own being, in our own hearts. 'God is the centre of my soul.' Now meditation is eminently practical because it requires each one of us to come to know 'from our own experience' what that statement means: 'God is the centre of my soul'.

We need to understand it, personally and profoundly, and to understand it as fact, not as poetry, not as theology. 'God is the centre of my soul.' The tragedy is that, far from understanding it, even theoretically, we think and act as if we ourselves were the centre. And we defend ourselves in the illusory centre of egoism. We look towards all reality as though we are at the centre. I'm sure we know well what a terrifying thing it is to discover the pure egoist, who has become fully convinced that he or she is at the centre of all reality. Equally, I hope we know what an inspiring and wonderful thing it is to find a person who is wise. What a wonderful thing it is to discover a saint, who knows and acts from the knowledge that God *is* the centre and that God invites us to be there with him through compassion, love, understanding, justice and true peace. The saint is one who has reality in sharp focus because he has God in sharp focus. Make no mistake about it, we are all called to this sanctity. The call is disturbing but it is made nonetheless. Everyone of us is called to have God in sharp focus. Everyone of us is called to the way of converting from the illusion of self-centredness to the reality of God-centredness. It is this sharp focus of reality that gives rise to the sympathy, sincere concern, the wide understanding, the compassion, and the practical love that should characterize Christ's disciples.

Never forget that it is the practice itself that leads us to the wisdom and holiness of this discipleship. All that is required is simply that we begin. All that is required of us this morning and this evening is that we say our mantra – as best we can – for the time of our meditation. It is no good just talking about it. It is no good just admiring it from a distance. The invitation is to get down to the daily discipline of our twice-daily meditation. What is the alternative? Without harmony, without holiness, there is panic. With panic there can be no peace and without peace there can be no justice.

Each of us must go beyond our personal panic to discover the full and profound confidence that comes from finding that we are founded on the rock who is Christ. The Good News of the New Testament is that we have no need to panic; we have no need to fear. We are invited to the supreme confidence that arises from supreme humility, which itself arises from our personal knowledge that, 'God is the centre of my soul'. Confidence leads to the peace of knowing that, when we have the first principle in first place, all the rest can follow naturally. And a life of faith becomes a life of affirmation:

The Son of God, Christ Jesus . . . was never a blend of Yes and No. With him it was, and is, Yes. He is the Yes pronounced upon God's promises, every one of them. That is why, when we give glory to God, it is through Christ Jesus that we say 'Amen'. And if you and we belong to Christ, guaranteed as his and anointed, it is all God's doing; it is God also who has set his seal upon us, and as a pledge of what is to come has given the Spirit to dwell in our hearts. (2 Cor 1:19–22)

St Paul's language possesses the supreme confidence that flows from knowing the reality that is beyond ourselves, the Spirit who dwells in our hearts. When we meditate we are being open to that Spirit, being open to the reality that is beyond ourselves. In that faith we are also being truly open to ourselves in the centre of our being where God is.

Two Words from the Past

One of the strengths we have to gain by meditating from within a tradition is that we can learn so much from the accumulated experience of the past. In the tradition that we speak from there are two words that can guide our day-to-day pilgrimage, and save us from unnecessary delays or diversions.

The early monastic Fathers soon discovered that one of the hurdles that every man and woman of prayer must surmount is what they described as *acedia*. *Acedia* is a fairly complex psychological concept, but it contains the notions of boredom, dryness, lack of satisfaction, a feeling of hopelessness, of not making progress. I think all of us are to some extent familiar with these manifestations of the ego. In fact, the concept of *acedia* is a particularly modern one. I think people in our society are very easily bored. (As a person who gives a lot of talks on the same subject I realize that myself very much). Boredom makes us restless and inconsistent in our commitments, all of us. Just as the early monks used to saunter off to Alexandria for a little bit of distraction from time to time, so we, in our secular society, are usually on the look-out for distraction. Those of us who have discovered the path of meditation will often feel a contrary tug, to withdraw our necks from the yoke so that we can rest up for a while. We all seek a diversion because we are getting a little tired with the sameness of the daily commitment to a pilgrimage that tests us with long periods of uneventfulness.

Only the other day a young man came to see me. He asked me, 'How can you bear to look out of your window and see the same thing every day? Doesn't it drive you mad?' Perhaps the real question should be, 'How is it we can always see so much, looking out of the same window every day?' The early Fathers knew that boredom comes from 'desire', the desire for fulfilment or fame, for something new, for a change of environment or activity, for different relationships, for a new toy, whatever it might be. Pure prayer shrinks desire. In the stillness of prayer, increasingly still as we approach the Source of all that is, of all that can be, we are so filled with wonder that there is no place for desire. It is not so much that we transcend desire but rather that there is simply no place in us any longer for such desire. All our space is being filled with the wonder of God. The attention that is scattered in desiring is recalled and absorbed in God.

Meditation, as you will all come to know from your own experience, is a discipline. It is the highest discipline of going beyond ourselves. This means going beyond our limitations as well as beyond all the toys or trifles that we could possibly imagine, into the sheer reality of God. The old monastic Fathers, seeing this as the goal, counselled their disciples to realize they could go beyond their *acedia*. We can go beyond despair, discontent and boredom by entering what they described as the state of *apatheia*. *Apatheia* is the second word the tradition offers us for encouragement.

We get our modern word 'apathy' from *apatheia* but it is not the meaning meant for us. In the meaning of the monastic elders it meant a state of detachment, a state wherein we are not possessed by our possessions, where we are not dominated by the desire to possess, to control. They saw that *apatheia* was a state of mind, a way of being and acting, that is absolutely necessary if we are going to love because it is only in this state of detachment that we do not try to *possess* or to control the other. We do not try to remake the other in our own image and likeness because we allow the other to be. And allowing them to be, we know them as they are and truly knowing them, we can only love them. The state of *apatheia*, of detachment, of passing beyond desire, is the state we enter in meditation. Meditating, we let go of the desire to control, to possess, to dominate. We seek instead only to be *who we are* and being the person we are, we are open to the God who is. It is as a result of that openness that we are filled with wonder and with the power and energy of God which is the power to be and the energy to be *in love*. When we are in love it is impossible to be bored. It is equally impossible to experience the other symptoms of *acedia*. Entering into this state however requires of us great generosity, the largeness and confidence to let go of our plans of our hopes, as well as of our fears and anxieties. We begin by doing this at the time of meditation so that we may be detached enough to be ourselves at all times, free enough to see beyond ourselves, to see who God is and who the person with us truly is. Seeing this, we are in love always.

The way to this detachment is the way of the mantra. It is the mantra and our faithfulness to it that loosens within us the roots of the ego that constantly leads us back into desire. In God's time the root is so loosened that it is plucked out and that is the moment of real wonder, the moment when each of us knows our true self and, knowing ourself, knows that we are in God.

> For the love of Christ leaves us no choice, when once we have reached the conclusion that one man died for all and therefore all mankind has died. His purpose in dying for all was that men, while still in life, should cease to live for themselves, and should live for him who for their sake died and was raised to life. With us, therefore, worldly standards have ceased to count in our estimate of any man; even if once they counted in our understanding of Christ, they do so now no longer. When anyone is united to Christ, there is a new world; the old order has gone, and a new order has already begun. (2 Cor. 5:14–17)

That is the purpose of our prayer, that we should each of us and all of us, be united to Christ.

At One with the Light

One of the words that is used to describe the purpose of meditation is 'enlightenment'. We meditate to become 'enlightened'. St John in his Gospel describes the purpose of the coming of Christ as being to banish the darkness. He speaks of the power of Christ's light as being to banish the darkness. He speaks of the power of his personal light as being so great that the darkness cannot overcome it, cannot quench it.

Yet we are all aware that there is still much darkness in our world. We hear every day of terrible injustices, of violence, of hatred, of feuds, of blind greed and insane destructiveness. We see all this at both the personal and political level, between our neighbours at home or abroad. Not so many of us however are aware of the residual darkness within ourselves. We need to recognize that we, too, have a dark side. We have a self-negating capacity to live at a level that we know is unworthy of our human destiny as persons who are images of God. When we begin to meditate, we soon come to understand that we cannot enter into the experience of meditation with just a part of our being. Everything that we are, the totality of our being, must be involved in this entry into wholeness itself, which realizes our own personal wholeness and harmony. Another way of expressing this is to say that every still-darkened part of our being must be open to the light. Every hidden part of us must come into the light. We do not meditate just to develop our religious side or our moral capacity. Meditation is the way into a harmonious integration of our total self with the whole of reality. A truly spiritual man or woman is in harmony with every capacity they possess. That is why the spiritual person does everything with the greatest possible spirit of perfection which leads to the greatest possible love and so to the greatest possible joy. The reason is this – meditation is not the process whereby we try to *see* the light. In this life we cannot see the light fully and continue to live. Our present concern should be for the light to see us, to search and know us; to be enlightened. Meditation is the process whereby we come *into* the light. As a natural consequence of this process we begin to see everything, the whole interlacing reality of life, by the power of the light. At this point we need to check our language. What is this 'light'? What does this great spiritual symbol mean? What is it that 'enlightens' us and changes the way we perceive daily reality? Jesus tells us that the power called 'light' is love. And so for the Christian meditator the test of our progress in meditation is simply how far we are moving into the enlightened state of seeing everyone and every inter-related thing by the light of God. Seeing by the light of his universal love makes us loving toward them all, too. Not judging, not rejecting, but seeing every person and, indeed, the whole of creation by this light we must discover love's source in our own heart. We must know ourselves loved: this is the knowledge of Christian enlightenment.

The way of meditation is simplicity itself. All we have to do is to make time available every morning and every evening of our life. For that time we must be open to the light, to God, to love. This will mean a radical conversion from egoistical, unenlightened consciousness. Not thinking our own thoughts, not constructing our own plans, we enter into an evermore profound silence, an evermore profound reverence of being, that is becoming rooted in God. Even our body is involved in this process. When we meditate alone or together we must make a serious effort to sit quite still, literally still for the whole period. This is a physical sign of the inner conversion. It is a certain *abandonment* of the body. Then, closing your eyes, gently begin to recite your word, your mantra. Recite it peacefully and calmly and allow the word to sink deep into your being while it builds up a resonance within you. Every part of your own being in resonance with God. The mantra realizes this reality. As we enter into that resonance we enter into the light of his love.

The astonishing thing about the Christian revelation, which is the message communicated to us by Jesus, is that everyone of us in every bus, every office building, every classroom, every home is called not only to see by the light, but our ultimate call is to see the light itself. At that moment we become indivisibly at one with the light. That is the moment when, as St Peter puts it, 'we share in the very being of God'. That is our actual destiny. We must begin to live that destiny now, to prepare for the fullness of it. The wonder and mystery of it transforms who we are now. And the purpose of our daily meditation is learning to live now, in this life, at every moment of our existence, in harmony with our ultimate, our eternal destiny. Daily meditation is our present preparation in time for a destiny that summons each of us to an infinity of expansion of spirit, an expansion into the pure joy of being.

Of course, we must always be careful not to be verbally intoxicated merely by talking about our destiny. We must take the practical steps to enter it. There is a strict limit to the benefit to be gained by reading books or listening to talks about meditation. The call is to enter into the experience now, today. Each of us must learn the simplicity, the humility, the poverty of spirit, to be content to say our word from the beginning to the end of our meditation. This will mean we will surrender *all* the thoughts including the most recurrent and pervasive ones: *Is this doing me any good? Am I getting anything out of it?* All self-centring has to go before we can launch out into the true centre of the depths of God's being.

When you begin you have to take this on faith. But if you say your mantra in that humble spirit, and if you say it every morning and every evening, from the beginning to the end, you will be led to understand now, in time, what eternal life is about. You will begin to understand the pure joy of being. You will begin to understand the sheer limitlessness of God's being. In God's infinity we find joy, and with joy, light.

The same God who said, 'Out of darkness let light shine', has caused his light to shine within us, to give the light of revelation – the revelation of the glory of God, in the face of Jesus Christ. (2 Cor. 4:6)

Fulfilment through Dispossession

It will help us to meditate more faithfully if we grow in perception of the reason why we should meditate. I think everybody alive is, in some degree of awareness, concerned with fulfilment and being content. Most of us start on the way to fulfilment by thinking in terms of acquiring things which make us content – whether it is knowledge or success, even perhaps spiritual knowledge and spiritual success. We can hardly help, in the kind of society that we live in, thinking of fulfilment in the materialistic sense of satisfaction and acquisition. This is how we *think* we will find contentment. But experience repeatedly proves otherwise: that the essence of fulfilment comes from discovering harmony, an agreement or resonance within yourself which radiates outwards to embrace and involve others and which indeed becomes a harmony with the whole universe. But before you uncover that harmony with everything that is created you must tread the path to the harmony that exists in your own heart. You must first discover that harmony within yourself, and that is the reason why we should meditate.

All of us know that it takes only a little experience to discover that success, possessions, wealth, respect, while perhaps good or useful in some ways are very limited. They have a restricted capacity to mediate to us the sort of fulfilment that comes when we discover how we are in resonance with the universe, with God as all in all. While revealing that resonance meditation makes a great demand. Do not have any false ideas about simplicity being easy or any illusions about instant breakthrough. There are no short cuts because there is no such thing as instant mysticism. Prayer is the heart of life and life is growth and growth is a process of change. Every one of us has to tread the path of conversion faithfully and with discipline. It is not that it is a path without joy, delight or wonder. But you will find that it is a path you have to be disciplined about; you have to be faithful to it to be able to accept its gifts. The problem with us as Westerners is to accept the way in all its simplicity. No greater simplicity exists than to accept a gift. To come to this simplicity of being, which is the condition of fulfilment, we have to uncomplicate ourselves. We have to begin where we are most complex, with our mental consciousness, our thinking. Meditation is a state of being where you are not thinking at all. You are not imagining. You are not having imaginary conversations or reviewing your past, present or future experience. You are in perfect peace, in perfect stillness of mind in a perfectly quiet imagination. The way to that stillness is the way that transcends thought and the whole process of imagination and ratiocination. Firstly, you have to want to find the way through these processes. If you do not, then meditation will seem unintelligible or threatening. Secondly, you have to want to find the way urgently enough to begin to follow it with commitment. Thirdly, when the Spirit guiding you so determines, you find the way. The way through is the simple repetition of a mantra.

The way towards the fulfilment that I am referring to is not to be seen as another kind of success. You cannot approach your meditation on the basis of success at all, because in meditation you are not seeking to achieve or acquire anything. Quite the reverse. You are seeking to lose and let go of everything. That aim is the most difficult idea for our Western minds to understand when we begin. It only takes a little reflection to realize that most of what we are renouncing we are happier without. But that reflection takes a little experience to consolidate. In the silence of meditation, when you go beyond thought and imagination, you begin to experience and later to understand that *being* is what life is about and that in meditation you are learning to *be*. To be is to live as the person you are, without trying to justify your existence or make excuses for your personality. Just to be, as you are. The wonder of it is that the more simple you become, the more you are able to enjoy to the full the gift of your being. But when you begin you have to begin in faith. You cannot come to meditation saying, 'If I can get something out of this I will do it for a trial run for three or six months'. You cannot come to it with demands. As St John of the Cross described it, 'The way to possession is the way of dispossession'. You have to let go of your thoughts, of your ideas, of your conscious and hidden ambitions and you have to *be*. The way to do it is to say your word. If all your attention is directed to saying your word and if you are neither lazy nor impatient, then gradually you are unhooked from all the thoughts and words and ideas and hopes and fears. You are free.

It is this liberation from the fear, the guilt and the ambition that are frozen into the complex mental structure of our thought and imagination, that allows you to be who you are without the *angst* of having to justify yourself. When you are meditating sit in the most comfortable, upright way that you can. Then close your eyes *gently*. When you are meditating every muscle in your face should be relaxed. Sometimes when people start you see them furrowing their brow and the expression on their face suggests they are determined to succeed at this even if it kills them. What you need is to let your facial muscles be as relaxed as possible. All the muscles in your body should relax. If you are sitting in the best way, your spine and shoulders are like a clothes hanger and your body is just drooped on those, just hanging absolutely erect, absolutely attentive, but completely relaxed and without tension.

Do not be looking for results. The only thing to look for is your own fidelity in being at your meditation in the morning and in the evening and, during your meditation, saying your word from beginning to end. That fidelity is the only way that you will learn to meditate. Forget results, to begin with at least, for the first twenty years or so. After that you will not be bothered about results anyway. This puts prayer in a very simple and practical context. But it all fits in to the overall Christian perspective, as expressed in what St Paul and the early Christians felt about the possibilities that are now, in

Christ, open to every one of us. This is why St Paul wrote this in his letter to the Ephesians:

> I kneel in prayer to the Father, from whom every family in heaven and on earth takes its name, that out of the treasures of his glory he may grant you strength and power through his spirit in your inner being. (Eph. 3:15–16)

Meditation is about meeting this strength and power by our encountering the Spirit who dwells in our hearts. St Paul ends this section by praying, 'so may you attain to fullness of being, the fullness of God himself'. The destiny of each one of us is to attain to that fulfilment of being and the way is to be fully open to the power of the Spirit of God in our heart.

Beyond Motivation

One of the primary things that we are all interested in is finding
our way not just to external harmony in our lives, where there
is no conflict or friction, but to an interior harmony, something
we can only describe by the word 'peace'. The sense of peace
is the sense of being intact, being together, being complete. It
is immensely more than the sense that one is becalmed. It is
transcendentally more than the absence of turbulence. It is
something much more positive. It is a sense of ecstatic well-
being. Peace flows in us when we have discovered our own
harmony in both external and interior dimensions. It is a
harmony within ourself as well as the harmony of which we are
capable through relationship with others and the harmony, for
example, that we can experience in nature, when you see the
mountains on a clear day or the sea in all its mighty moods. In
those harmonious moments of revelation it flashes in on one
that this is what humanity is about: a sense of oneness with
nature, with oneself, with others. That is why we meditate. It
is a sad and dangerous person who dismisses these moments as
sentimental or escapist. Peace is not an escape from the
struggles of life. It is the struggles of life honourably completed.

When you begin to meditate you have to have some motivation. You have to have an objective to get you going, a push
as it were to start you on the road. There is no better incentive
than to achieve this state of inner and outer harmony. Peace
is a noble objective and a unifying one. In many of the sacred
scriptures of both the eastern and western traditions this goal
is described as the state of *blessedness*, of *glory*, of *salvation*,
or simply of *life*. The sense is of being fully, humanly alive. So,
if you want a motivation to meditate that would be as good a

reason as any. But once you start to meditate on a regular daily basis in your life you will begin to realize that soon meditation operates by its own dynamic. It is not necessary to be constantly asserting or defining your motivation or goal. There is a directional impulse in meditation itself which carries you forward with less and less self-prodding or external encouragement. It is simply unlike any other activity in your life. You do not approach it in the conventional way that would say, 'If I meditate so many times then I will get this return, x-level of peacefulness, and if I am particularly faithful then I will get to x plus one'.

Once you start to meditate you realize that you come to it with a decreasing amount of demands and without looking for any payoff. We meditate simply because this is the clearest way that we can find to lead us to the sense of wholeness, of oneness, which is beyond our control or possession and which can only be enjoyed once we accept its nature as gift. In meditation we discover that the acceptance of this gift is what life is given to us for, to be whole, to be one, and thus to activate all the potential that is freely ours for life, for happiness, for being. Meditating is to the spirit just what breathing is to the body. If someone asks you what is your motivation for breathing, you would have to reply, 'I have no motivation except to live. It is necessary to breathe because it is necessary for life. I have no conscious motivation for it at all'. The longer you meditate, the more you experience your spirit to be in peaceful harmony with your body, your own whole being to be in peaceful harmony with all creation and with your Creator. You will increasingly realize that you do not need any motivation for meditating. You meditate because you are, and because God is, because that is the structure of reality, and because that is what you are meant to realize: God the Creator and myself the creature, alive in God's creation. Meditation is simply the way to become wholly alive to that all-encompassing reality.

Before you sit down to meditate each day remember that the purpose of it all is to lose all self-consciousness. We are not bothered about creating or projecting the right sort of image to anyone. We are only concerned with being, being who we are, where we are. To be at peace is to accept the gift of being and in accepting it to lose our self-consciousness in the divine mind.

It sometimes happens that as you are meditating, particularly when you are beginning, a great feeling of peacefulness overtakes you. Then you say to yourself, 'This is rather marvellous. Where is this going to lead me? What is this about? Let me experience this'. You stop saying your mantra and the great likelihood is that as soon as you do it the sense of peace has gone or becomes a memory. But there is usually worse to come because, having lost the sense of peace, you are determined to try and recapture it again. So you start saying your mantra more loudly or more intensely, more self-consciously to try to possess once more that feeling of peace. But meditation, as St John of the Cross described it, is a way of dis-possession. You are not trying to possess peace or God, or to get him to give graces, consolation, or a high of some kind. We are not asking for *anything*. We are meditating because it is necessary that we should meditate and so we meditate without demands, renouncing every sort of materialistic objective. The only true motive for meditation is the ultimate one – that we meditate to *be*. To be the person we are called to be in the Christian vision is a very wonderful vocation. The person we are called to be is a free person accepting fully and responding fully to the gift of our own creation. More than that it is to be a person accepting and responding fully to the gift of our own salvation, the fullness of life given to us in Jesus. Even more than that, we meditate as our response to our own renewed nature as temples of the Holy Spirit. That is what each of us is, the resting place of God's Holy Spirit.

This is what Christian prayer is about. It is not about asking God for things or informing God about things. It is about being wholly open to him, wholly with him, wholly in harmony with him. Meditation *is* peace, it *is* happiness and it *is* total security and liberty because in it we are anchored in total reality. And God is anchored in us through the humanity of Jesus. St Paul proclaimed this universal enlightenment:

For the same God who said, 'Out of darkness let light shine', has caused his light to shine within us, to give the light of revelation – the revelation of the glory of God in the face of Jesus Christ. (2 Cor. 4:6)

That is our motivation to meditate, because the glory of God is to be found in our hearts. It *is* found if only we will be still and silent and poor. Our poverty consists in this, that we surrender all words, all thoughts, all imagination and we stay with the one word, the word of our mantra, and that we are utterly faithful to the recitation of it from the beginning to the end.

Meditation and the Way of Work

To learn to meditate is to begin the process of making contact, vital contact, with the source of all being, the source of all life and the source of all energy. What we have to discover is that this creative source is to be found within our own being, life and energy. That is the great teaching of Jesus: the Kingdom of heaven is within you. To meditate is simply to begin to live in full harmony with the power that has called us into being and which is the power that has called everyone and everything into being. As you know, the process of meditation is very simple. Choose a quite place, a quiet time, sit still and say your mantra, Maranatha.

What each of us discovers is that this precious time of peace and silence each day will gradually affect every area of our life. One of the first things we learn is really to *listen* and then we begin to understand there is a deeper reality, a deeper significance to persons, to things, to events, than appears on the surface. One of the areas that our meditation affects is our work. The kind of work we do and above all the way we do our work is of enormous importance for all of us. Meditation is a great preparation for our work. And done well, our work is a great preparation for meditation. In meditation we learn to lose ourselves in God. We learn to take the focus of attention off ourselves and to concentrate our attention on the source of all. And in work we have an opportunity again to lose ourselves, to do our work for its own sake, so that we lose all sense of ourselves. We forget our satisfaction, our enjoyment, and we learn to let the work stand by itself and be its own reason for being. Now this is difficult for us to understand as modern people because most of us in our society have such an ego-centred approach to work. But the essential thing about creative energy is that it be turned out beyond itself. The watchmaker is lost in his watch, the painter is lost in his art. Creative energy turned inwards is egoism and in meditation as we say our mantra, all our energy, our whole being is turned out, beyond itself into the centre of the divine energy itself. And just reflect for a moment what that means for each of us. It means that all our small, personal joys, cares, worries, fears – all of them are lost in the divine energy which is love. What all of us need, wherever we are on the pilgrimage, is to expand into love. And meditation is our great opportunity to go beyond self into the heart of the mystery of God.

Every life has a divine significance. Every life has a divine potential. In meditating we open our lives to that significance and to that potential and in that opening we are swept beyond ourselves into the creative energy of God. The way is the way of humility, to say our word and to say it faithfully and to say it every morning and every evening. It is the way of simplicity, to surrender complexity, to surrender dividedness and to stay with the divine oneness of God. And it is the way of faithfulness, of constancy. We are faithful to our own destiny in God. We are faithful to the realization that we can only be in God. Listen to St Peter:

> So come to him, our living Stone – the stone rejected by men but choice and precious in the sight of God. Come, and let yourselves be built, as living stones, into a spiritual temple; become a holy priesthood, to offer spiritual sacrifices acceptable to God, through Jesus Christ . . . you are a chosen race, a royal priesthood, a dedicated nation, and a people claimed by God for his own. . . You are now the people of God, who once were not his people; outside his mercy once, you have now received his mercy. (1 Pet. 2:4–5, 9–10)

As a royal priesthood, every time we meditate, we do what St Peter is speaking about. We come into the presence of God and let ourselves be built as living stones into a spiritual temple.

Cosmic Poverty

Some years ago when I was first giving talks on meditation I showed a talk I was preparing to one of my confreres in London. When he came back to see me, his face looked very serious. He said, 'This isn't *all* there is, surely?' I said, 'Well, it is, actually'. But he said, 'You have some funny stories to put in, haven't you?' I said, 'Well, no, I hadn't thought of putting any in'. So he said, 'If you give that talk as it is, I can assure you that everyone will walk away in absolute despair'. I was reminded of this when I was in Manchester last week when the man who runs our groups there, and who had a rather protective attitude towards me, came up to me just as I was going on to the platform to give the talk and said, 'You will put in a few funny stories, Father, won't you?' My confrère in London had gone on to say. 'Well if you aren't going to tell any funny stories, at least warn them before you give the talk'. So that is really what this preamble is about.

So let us begin this very serious reflection on poverty by thinking of these strengthening words of St Paul:

> May he strengthen you, in his glorious might, with ample power to meet whatever comes with fortitude, patience and joy; and to give thanks to the Father who has made you fit to share the heritage of God's people in the realm of light. (Col. 1:11–12)

The qualities of the spiritual path St Paul describes here can help us to see the poverty, which is our need for God's strength, as the essential ground for compassion. A Christian above all needs to see meditation as the way of compassion. It is so important for us to understand that our call is to gentleness.

59

The Christian revelation is of a doctrine of redemption, of forgiveness; that we are redeemed from our faults, from our imperfections, from our stupidity and that we are *already* forgiven. It is not that God just forgets. He forgives. Before we can experience this each one of us must understand that we are sinners. That means that each of us has our own brand of illusion that we weave. The call to compassion is answerable when we realize that we are, all of us, redeemed by a real love that dispels illusion and is so great that it will undergo any manner of suffering.

The physical and mental sufferings of the passion of Christ seem terrible to us but it has always struck me that perhaps his deepest suffering was his apparent inability to communicate his love to those around him. They were so slow to understand, not just the personal, universal redemptive message that he was speaking to them, but the personal love that he was offering them. They stayed set in their ways of egoism, stupidity and self-protection. Now the way of meditation is, by contrast with egoism, a way of entering into our own powerlessness. When we meditate, in saying the mantra, we enter into our own utter poverty. And in that apparent nothingness we become one with all. It is as though we enter a cosmic poverty because everywhere we look we see the same utter poverty. This is the poverty of the passion and suffering of Christ and the triumph of the cross is that this suffering, this love, has overcome the darkness. It has negated the negativity. The wonder of meditation is that this cosmic power which has driven back our own egoistical darkness, this power of triumphant love, is to be found in our own hearts. We do indeed encounter the power and the energy of love on our pilgrimage. But it is not the kind of power that could give rise to pride, to hubris, to intolerance. It is a power that we can only discover in utter darkness. It is a power we can only discover in utter poverty. And that is why it is a power that gives rise to deep compassion and to a capacity to enter into the suffering of another, of all others. Even more than that, the call to all Christians is to mediate this love because it is a love that, through us, has the power to redeem the suffering of others. In that sense we are truly co-redeemers with Christ once we uncover his love within us. Having discovered it we already know that we all come from the same darkness, from the same nothingness. We know too that all of us have been delivered from it by an infinite love.

The practicality of the message of Christian meditation is that by our fidelity to the pilgrimage and by our openness to the indwelling love we come to understand that the great work in life is to communicate this love, to help others to see by its light. If we ourselves understand this and see and judge everything by the light of this love, then we have learned to live our lives with supreme compassion. The way of meditation is at the same time the way of compassion, of simplicity and of joy. Only one thing is necessary for us to follow this way and that is to tread the pilgrimage with utter seriousness, not half-heartedly but whole-heartedly and single-mindedly. The Christian mystery has always called us to this wholeness and perfect sincerity, where our poverty leads to the riches of the Kingdom and a life lived in active goodness of every kind.

> We ask God that you may receive from him all wisdom and spiritual understanding for full insight into his will, so that your manner of life may be worthy of the Lord and entirely pleasing to him. We pray that you may bear fruit in active goodness of every kind, and grow in the knowledge of God. May he strengthen you, in his glorious might, with ample power to meet whatever comes with fortitude, patience and joy; and to give thanks to the Father who has made you fit to share the heritage of God's people in the realm of light. (Col. 1:9–12)

To enter the realm of the enlightened is our call and we respond to it by entering into our own heart. By entering our own poverty we learn to live our entire lives out of the infinite riches of God.

Seeing Through Our Selves

Consider these words of St Peter:

> In his own person he carried our sins to the gibbet, so that we might cease to live for sin and begin to live for righteousness. (1 Pet 2:24)

Meditation is the great way of purification. Every time we say our mantra, we purify, we clarify our spirit. The process of meditation over a lifetime is the restoration of our spirit to its natural translucency. So often, when we look into our spirit, we see only ourselves. Our spirit is like a mirror and all we see is our own reflection. But the glass must be cleared and cleansed. It is as though the other side of the glass is covered with the sum total of the dross and trivia of a lifetime, with all the images that we have accumulated. Meditation is a cleansing of the glass so that when we look *at* it we see right *through* it. We see reality unimpeded by any reflection of ourselves. We have to meditate every day, every morning and evening, because we are always accumulating more limiting dross and images. The wonder of the life of Jesus and his message to us is that our spirit need not be constrained by any limits whatsoever. Each of us is called to unlimited development, to expansion and to utter freedom as we soar to total union with God.

The daily meditation is of such importance because we must ensure that our spirit is always cleansed, always polished. Ultimately – such is the mystery within which we live our lives and have our being – the glass itself is shattered and we are then in direct contact with reality. I wonder why it is that so many people are afraid to set out on this path. I think it must be because we live in an age of fear. The extraordinary phenomenon of our time is the nameless fear that haunts people. There are so many people adrift in their lives, without signposts, without standards. They live in a world in which they feel that anything goes, old rules seem outdated and old systems of thought or theology seem irrelevant. The result is that we are left with a haunting fear of rootlessly wondering where we are, where we are going and what will happen next. Meditation is a return to being rooted in essential reality. A return to our spirit. A return to the base from which we can come into direct contact with the basic structure of reality. Meditation is a return to God. Though, of course, it is not a return. It is a striving forward. It is a pilgrimage of purification that has as its result the fact that we are no longer trapped or limited by mirror images. It is of such supreme importance because it is the journey beyond fear. In making contact with our own spirit and then in going beyond ourselves into the mystery of God, all fear is left behind.

If you think of all the natural disasters that can occur – famine, earthquakes, floods, tornadoes – there is something obvious that we can do to address all of them. But a person or a group or a nation possessed by fear is on the road to insanity, blind to the obvious. For a symbol of all this, you have only to look at the present political situation between East and West: you see the great Russian power, fearing freedom in its own empire, fearing attack from the West; you see the West filled with fear of the Russian power and of its own moral incoherence. In between these two fear-blocks you see the country of Poland crushed and abused. This fear must be cast out, and it can only be cast out by love. And the fear is of such mammoth proportions that it can only be cast out by infinite love. That is why we must find men and women who will accept the discipline of prayer, the discipline of the pilgrimage of meditation, who will make contact with the God who is love, who will be energized by his power of love and who will communicate it wherever they go.

When we meditate, we turn away from all illusion, from all images, from all fear, and we turn to God himself. We start by returning to our own heart and the extraordinary thing is that,

63

as we are filled with his glory, with his love, there is no longer any place for us to stand, even in our own hearts. In meditation we are truly lost in the light of his glory, and it is when we are lost in that light that we become the light. There is a lot of darkness in our world. It is in desperate need of light, of men and women of light. And our pilgrimage of selflessness, which is also one of discipline, is a pilgrimage into the light. That is why when we meditate we must learn the discipline to sit perfectly still and to say the mantra with perfect attention: to leave everything of self behind. We must come to the place where we have no place. We must come directly to the light so that we become the light. Listen to St Peter again: Whoever loves life . . . must turn from wrong and do good, seek peace and pursue it. (1 Pet. 3:10, 11)

To meditate is to have life, to be converted, to seek peace, not just for ourselves but for all.

Created to be Light

In the central spiritual tradition, God is seen as pure light and the spiritual path itself is seen as the 'path of enlightenment', a coming in to that light. The Godless world of materialism on the other hand is a world full of shadows. Each of our possessions throws a shadow and creates an area of darkness in and around us. But there is, in all of us, a spiritual sense that reminds us that we were created for light not shadow, for freedom not possession. We were created to become light, to *be* light. In the tradition that teaches us, God is pure light 'in whom there is no darkness' because he is all-subject. It is objects that throw shadows. We must understand that we are each called to be 'pure subject'. We are called to be 'one' with Him, neither objectified nor objectifying. The way of meditation is a way of enlightenment, a way of entering fully and definitively into God's pure light. In meditation, pure prayer as the tradition calls it, neither God nor we are objects.

The way is simplicity itself. The essence of the teaching is to say the mantra continuously and, as you will discover if you begin, we will have to take responsibility to keep the purity of that doctrine absolutely clear so that we do not muddy it, through laziness or compromise. We do not need to complicate it. Choose your word and recite your word from the beginning to the end of your meditation. All the rest is pure gift and will be given to you. We become *giveable-to*, because meditation is a way of detachment. We must not become ensnared in the world of objects, regardless of whether they are material or mental objects. Remember, and keep this clear in your minds and hearts that our call is to pure intersubjectivity. We are called to be one with the One who *is*, the One who is all light.

Coming out from the shadows can be a painful business. We all have our favourite hiding places where we can take refuge, where we can go when we want to rest up for a bit. But coming into the light is a surrendering of all those hiding places because we take as our one place of rest, the pure light of the Lord God. We need to be very simple about this, very childlike. Don't complicate. Simplify.

All examples and metaphors have their hazards. We are not talking here about the glaring light of an arc lamp throwing out a cruel, all-white light, relentless, merciless. When we speak of God as light we are speaking of a gentle, all-pervasive, always pure light that enlightens and enlivens everything that is bathed in its rays. It is a light that is both bright and warm. It is above all a light that reveals reality as love and as we come into the light we recognize its personal oneness, its wholeness facing us. We will recognize, too, that by remaining in the light we will see our own being, for the light enables us to see everything as it truly is. Our temptation is to try to analyse the light, to break it up into its constituent parts in the spectrum.

Analysis and reductionism are disastrous attitudes in prayer because they assume that the whole is made up of its parts, that partiality comes first and wholeness is built up from it. Faith, on the other hand, goes deeper than analysis, trusting that the whole is anterior to its particular expressions. As soon as we start concentrating on – thinking about – a specific attribute of God in prayer we have left the experience of God as he is in himself, that is in his wholeness and indivisible simplicity.

The invitation that we each of us are given is to see the light whole and entire because our invitation is to see what is, whatever is, in its wholeness and entirety. Learning to stay within the light is what meditation is about. The light that enlightens teaches us that God is all. The light that enlightens teaches us that we can only really be when we are in God, for he is all there is.

This is what we learn to see clearly in the brightness of the light, that God is, that God is all and that God is love. Remember the way. The way is to stop thinking. The way is to stop imagining. Close down the processes of the mind and be silent and attentive. The way to that fully awakened, wholly conscious silence, the way to that closing down of all the operations of the mind is to learn to say your mantra. To learn to say the mantra we need to be humble, to be patient. We need to understand that it will take time, that there will be false starts. There will inevitably be failures when you will give up. But don't worry about any of that. The only thing that matters is to start again. To keep starting is to be on the way, to be on the pilgrimage.

The Christian Scandal

Recently I re-read the Letter to the Ephesians and I was especially struck again by these words:

> So shall we all at last attain to the unity inherent in our faith and our knowledge of the Son of God – to mature manhood, measured by nothing less than the full stature of Christ. (Eph 4:13)

As well as reading the New Testament I read a copy of *Time* or *Newsweek* that was in the house. A considerable section of the magazine was devoted to the scandal at the Vatican bank. It struck me as I read this unsavoury story that a scandal at the Vatican is really as nothing, compared with the scandal that we ourselves contribute to; namely that we are, as a body of Christians, so slow to come to what St Paul calls the 'unity inherent in our faith'. Why are we so slow? Simply because the only way to come to that unity is to leave self behind. The real Christian scandal is that we hear and even preach this message but are so slow and reluctant to respond to it. This is a scandal infinitely greater than a few hundred million dollars missing here and there.

Meditation is so important for us because it is a way of actual response that leads us away from self. It is a way of transcendence. It is a way of entering into the reality that is greater than ourselves. It is a way that brings us into that liberty of spirit that arises when we are no longer thinking about ourselves, our plans, our self-development and our fulfilment. While meditating we have only one consideration, which is to enter into a state of harmonious resonance with the divinising energy of God. In the Christian vision the energy of God is limitless, free, self-communicating love. In the Christian revelation, this is the call that each of us has, to allow that love to become *the* supreme reality in our lives.

Consider all the innumerable things that can go wrong in our lives. Then reflect what can undo these catastrophes? What can heal the inevitable wounds? In every case the answer is 'the power of love'. Love it is that heals, that makes new, that fills us with hope, that delivers us from the prison of our own egoism. In meditation we learn to be still, to be calm, to be recollected and to become aware of the love of God's presence in our hearts. This awareness arises from his revelation not our manipulation. What we have to do though, is to be still. His presence is not just another theory, some speculative theology. It is a dynamic personal presence that is to be found in the heart of each one of us, found if only we will be still. Stillness is the door through which we enter the state of transcendence that leads us into the greater reality. Forgetting about ourselves and encountering this reality, entering into this presence is, quite simply, *the* most important thing in our lives. It is the supreme priority of each day and of each phase in our life because, once we do set out on this path, every part of our life becomes energized with the divine love and this means that we are constantly healed. We are coming into a state of inherent unity. We are constantly being made whole and as a result we are continually discovering new courage to go on living with hope in the goodness of God, and with supreme confidence in his plan being worked out in our lives.

We need to be more conscious of the destiny that is given to us by God, and more courageous in responding to it. Very often we cannot see this. It seems as though we are subject to quite arbitrary forces at work in our lives. But the plan is there and the plan for each of us is that we should come to that maturity, measured by nothing less than the fullness of Christ. Meditation helps to centre us in the heart of the divine mystery and from this standpoint we see ourselves from within the divine mystery itself – a radical new self-knowledge purified of the self-centredness of egoism. The astonishing thing about our vocation, our uniquely personal call, is that from this standpoint of God-centredness we see God, others and ourselves with a new perspective, a perspective that recognizes God as the universal centre and so aligns everything else upon him. This perspective is of enormous practical importance for us because it helps us to live daily from an understanding of the mystery of our own creation, the mystery of the gift of our own life. Equally important is to understand the very consoling fact that simply *being* in the presence of God is itself a healing experience. Prayer, which is the experience of presence, is itself an experience of calm confidence that takes us to a peace beyond ourselves in the realization of personal wholeness, of completion with others. In meditation we learn that in him we are in all senses made one. This oneness is the source of all hope, all confidence and all compassion because we know with a certainty of knowledge that all things are destined to find their resolution in him, with him and through him.

Let me remind you again of the necessity for faithfulness, in particular for the daily faithfulness to your meditation, whatever the difficulties (and they are often considerable); and your faithfulness, too, during the time of meditation to the recitation of the mantra. It is this simplicity, this faithfulness, that leads us directly into the fullness of the mystery which is the mystery of our own destiny, the mystery of the self-revelation of God and the mystery of the love of God in Jesus. Touching this mystery in our hearts changes our lives and as St Paul knew, it can change the world.

> Be most careful then how you conduct yourselves: like sensible men, not simpletons. Use the present opportunity to the full, for these are evil days. Do not be fools, but try to understand what the will of the Lord is. Do not give way to drunkenness and the dissipation that goes with it, but let the Holy Spirit fill you: speak to one another in psalms, hymns and songs; sing and make music in your hearts to the Lord; and in the name of our Lord Jesus Christ give thanks every day for everything to our God and Father. (Eph. 5:15–20)

All or Nothing

The power of the New Testament lies in its dramatic sense of the contrast between life before faith in Christ and life as transformed by that faith. St Peter saw it as being as dramatic as the contrast between death and life.

> Why was the Gospel preached to those who are dead? In order that, although in the body they received the sentence common to men, they might in the spirit be alive with the life of God. (1 Pet 4:6)

That is exactly what our meditation is for – to pass from the death of half-life to being fully alive in the Spirit with the life of God. We should never underestimate or be embarrassed by the full magnificence of the Christian vision and the Christian invitation. In meditation we live by that vision and accept the invitation because meditation is a total availability to God. When we meditate, when we sit for those half hours, in the simplicity of saying our mantra, we are wholly available to God, totally at his disposition. This is what pure prayer is about: no demands, no recriminations, no playacting, no threats, just a simple, total availability to the wonder of the ultimate reality. Meditation is important for us because by means of this availability it leads us into the experience of faith.

It is not just that we believe in God or even that we try to live by the belief in his love. It is knowing that we are in him and he is in us and that this is what living the life of God's love means. Knowing it personally in the depths of our own being is what we gain in meditation, and this knowledge is real. There is all the difference between knowledge that is purely speculative and knowledge that is wholly experiential. Speculative knowledge has its own place and is useful in its own time and then it is wholly good. It can bring us deep intellectual understanding and deep intellectual pleasure but it always remains at the level of the speculative, of the theoretical. Experiential knowledge, on the other hand, involves us as complete persons. We are not just dealing in abstractions. We are not thinking of God as First Cause or Prime Mover. The wonder of our meditation is that we are intimately involved in the personal mystery of God. The very fact of our creation invites us into the 'inner court' of love. There we find ourselves lost in God. Speculation is important, even deep speculation about God is important. It *is* useful to try to reflect about the Trinity, to understand the terms that traditional theology has used, like processions of persons, the doctrine of circumincession and the Divine Kenosis. But that is not the essence of the Christian invitation. The core of the Christian way is experiential not speculative, interior not objective.

Both speculation – looking at experience in the mirror of the mind and reflecting on it through images and ideas – and experience – being simply present and involved unselfreflectedly – are expressions of faith. We think and we pray because we have faith. But the ultimate value of our thought depends upon the depth and vitality of prayer. Thought will not lead us to the experience itself. Only pure faith will cross the threshold. We are united with and we are meant to begin to experience, however dimly, 'in this life', as St Peter puts it, the torrent of love that is the internal dynamism of the Trinity. The experience at present must be but a dim apprehension of the reality, because none of us could continue to live if the fullness of the power of love were let loose within us. But the experience is not just a brief epiphany that comes and goes. All our thought and action are capable of being touched and transfigured by the experience; because the experience is constant, eternal. It is conscious for us when, in prayer, we become present to it. The daily experience of meditation then brings us ever more deeply into the constant conviction that becomes the all-pervasive conviction of our lives that God is one. He is supreme intelligence and supreme power by being all-embracing love.

But that is not all. There is also the extra-ordinary knowledge that it is our destiny, the destiny of each one of us to enter into his dynamism of oneness in complete peace and total silence, and in that peace and silence to know ourselves loved. After this we know forever that love is the supreme reality. The peace of this entry into God we can accept easily enough. But it is the silence we all find so much more difficult. As we enter ever deeper into the depths of silence, we are tempted to return to the shallows, to postpone the ultimate leap, the total act of faith. And perhaps we are right to be hesitant, because once made that leap is made forever. There is no turning back from the leap of 'all or nothing'.

The Old Testament recognized our God to be a 'jealous' God, a 'devouring fire' because he cannot abide half measures or duplicity. In the New Testament we find the way to over-come the inconstancy and half-measures of human commit-ment: discipleship of Christ. The way to be open to his infinity, to his infinite love, is for our finite hearts to be wholly open to Jesus. All our capacity is needed for this tremendous process of self-opening which is a journey into silence, into apparent nothingness, but also a journey into the All, who is one, who we name God. The way to make this journey is the faithful way of the mantra. We are not to say our mantra half-heartedly or for just some of the time – our God is a jealous God – but to say it with complete fidelity. In generously leaving behind the thoughts, the words, the memories and daydreams, all imagination and all self-imaging we go courageously into the silence, into the peace and so into the oneness of God.

Kissing the Joy as it Flies

Meditation is concerned with detachment. And as in our Western religious vocabulary there is no word more misunderstood than *detachment*, meditation can often present unnecessary problems or complications for people. It seems to us, generally, that detachment means a frosty sort of platonic indifference and it was this that put most of us off the idea when we came across the word in many spiritual books of the past which talked of Christian life from a largely negative or repressive view of detachment. Yet I feel that detachment is the most important lesson that meditation has to teach us today as men and women of the West, affected by this often badly-emphasized religious culture.

Detachment is not dissociation from yourself or an evasion of your problems or your responsibilities. It is not a denial of friendship or affection, or even of passion. Detachment is, in essence, detachment from self-preoccupation, from that often unconscious mind-set that puts *myself* at the centre of all creation. Detachment is equally concerned with a commitment to friendship, to enduring brotherhood and sisterhood, to a self-transcending and outreaching love. Detachment makes love possible because love is only possible if we are detached from self-preoccupation, if we have moved out of self-isolation, if we are freed from self-indulgence. The disengagement that detachment involves is from using other people for one's own ends. But above all, and this is the important lesson we have to learn in meditation, detachment is liberation from the anxiety we have about *my own* survival as a self. Life teaches us all that loving is in essence losing oneself in the larger reality of the other, of others, and of God. Detachment from self-

centredness liberates us for love so that we are no longer dominated by the animal quest for survival. Detachment requires
fully human trust: trust of the other, both in other people and
in God. It requires the willingness to let go, to give up controlling, and to *be*.

In meditation, by learning to say your mantra, you learn to
trust, you learn to be. Indeed the joy of meditation is that it
is a celebration of being, a celebration of sheer joy in receiving
your life as gift, and doing what Blake called kissing 'the joy
as it flies'. Prayer is not possessing, not controlling but sheer
celebration of being. We come to this celebration because meditation leads us to centredness, to the still point. In each person
there is a still point that is me but is not *exclusively* me. What
you will learn from your own experience in meditation is that
there is only one centre, which is the centre in all centres. This
is the understanding we come to in meditation, again out of
our own experience, of the profound unity of being, the unity
that is in us and the unity in which we have our being. The
commitment in meditation is to be detached from self-conscious
preoccupation, through fidelity to the mantra during the meditation itself, and to the twice-daily practice of this *discipline* of
detachment. The times of meditation, then, become progressively more simple, more joyous, more centred. And our lives,
which are deeply changed through meditation, reveal from our
own experience what it means to say 'God is love'. The centre
of all centres is the God who is love.

Christian discipleship is lived detachment and loving other-
centredness. And discipleship begins with a call that awakens
us out of the coma of self-preoccupation. We are called, we
are chosen. Meditation is our response to that call from the
deepest centre of our awakened consciousness.

> You did not choose me: I chose you. . . This is my command-
> ment to you: Love one another. (Jn 15:16, 17)

In meditation by letting go, by openness to the centre of being
we learn how to love.

Christ's Birth in Us

As we prepare each year for the feast of Christmas we have a precious opportunity to reflect upon the marvellous context in which the Christian vision lets us see we live. The Incarnation, the birth of Jesus, is the revelation of God. It is the showing of his power, his wisdom, his love in the man Jesus. The Incarnation is like a pouring out of God on earth and, as the life of Jesus proves, God holds nothing back. The generosity of God is incarnated in the generosity of Jesus. In his life we see his availability to the crowds, his compassion for the sick, for the mourning. His utter selflessness, we know, comes to a climax in his death on the cross.

Meditating is our way to that same generosity. It is difficult for any of us to be generous. It is difficult for us all to be selfless. And yet there is nothing of real advantage to be found in meanness and selfishness, which we all know through the pain of discovering meanness and selfishness in ourselves. But the Incarnation – God becoming Man – is an encouragement to us to grow in generosity. It is also a comfort to us because we know that Jesus, as a fellow human being, understands our fear, the reserved and timorous approach we have when it comes to the moment of total commitment. Our self-protective approach is understood by him as we fearfully discover the absoluteness involved in responding to Christ. This is why meditation is so important because meditation is itself an absolute commitment. It is a commitment to be open to Christ totally, unreservedly, by taking the attention off ourselves and putting it on him. And the way we do this needs to be a very simple way if we are to circumvent our resistance and reluctance to give everything. There is no way simpler than the mantra.

This is a way of absolute commitment. Either you recite it or you do not. You can follow your own thoughts; you can make your own plans; you can analyse your own insights when you are meditating. But if you do, you will soon learn from your own experience that you remain in the closed system of self-consciousness. Whereas reciting the mantra and continuing to recite it, is letting go of your own thoughts, fears, sadness and planning. This multi-levelled letting go releases us into the liberty of the infinity of God. There is no such thing as a partial release. We are not partially redeemed by a partial incarnation. You either leap or you stay where you are. The call of Christian discipleship is to trust and follow Jesus, not by half measures but in absolute measure. In his gentleness, however, he gives us a path that leads us by a steady progression, away from self into his infinite mystery. That is the path we follow as we meditate.

Christ was born at Bethlehem and that is a marvellous, historical fact. But it is a fact that is completed. It was completed in the past so that now he must be born in our hearts. Our hearts must be made ready for him. There must be room for him in the inn of our heart. That is all meditation is: a readying and opening of our heart for the birth of Christ. And it is because he is the infinite God that we must let go of everything else, so that there is space for him in our hearts. The mystery is that when he is come to birth in our hearts, everything is come to birth with him. Our hearts are filled with all his love, all his compassion, all his forgiveness. We know ourselves forgiven, loved and understood by the infinite God and by his Son, our brother. Filled with this experiential knowledge we cannot fail to communicate and share it with anyone to whom we turn, with whom our lives are interwoven.

Meditation is a daily commitment to these truths, not as theory but in practice; not as a philosophy of life but as our daily experience of leaving self behind to be open to God, in his Son, Jesus, by the power of the Spirit.

> There can be no other foundation beyond that which is already laid; I mean Jesus Christ Himself. . . Surely you know that you are God's temple, where the Spirit of God dwells. (1 Cor. 3:11.16)

That is the clear understanding of the early Church. The foundation of our journey to God is the self-giving of God in the Incarnation and we must come to know that God's self-knowledge, his Spirit, dwells in us. We find ourselves made real as his temples, made whole on the rock that is Jesus Christ. The way of meditation seems to the world foolish. That we do leave behind thoughts, images and words because of our faith in this reality of Christ is the foolishness of divine wisdom. We leave behind limited, finite thoughts and words to be open to the unlimited love of God in Jesus. The absoluteness of God's gift makes fools of us all:

> Make no mistake about this: if there is anyone among you who fancies himself wise – wise, I mean, by the standards of this passing age – he must become a fool to gain true wisdom. (1 Cor. 3:18)

Saying the mantra, morning and evening, every day of our life is a way of foolishness in the eyes of the world. But it leads to the only wisdom there is: full consciousness in the consciousness of Jesus.

The Process of Reduction

One of the things that the feast of Christmas brings to mind is the extraordinary mystery of God reduced almost to nothing as he takes on human form. Here we contemplate the deep mystery which requires that before something great can be accomplished, there has to be this preceding process of reduction. It is the process whereby all the energy is concentrated in something minute, in order that it can burst the bonds of limitation. And this is exactly what the Incarnation is about. It is about God in Jesus, taking on all our human limitations and accepting them by becoming a man like us. So he starts the process whereby all our bonds, our limitations are burst and are, in fact, definitively overcome forever, all in the person of Jesus, through the human consciousness of Jesus. This process is, as St Paul put it, God emptying himself out, into Jesus, pouring the divine essence into the person of Jesus Christ.

You do not have to be meditating for very long to know that this liberating reduction is exactly the process of meditation. Meditation, when you begin, is very evidently a process of reduction. We give up thinking, we give up discursive, wandering thought. We renounce imagination, we even turn from our better insights. All this is a process of reduction. It is a process of limiting everything in our minds, for that supreme moment of concentration when we are available for one experience alone. We are preparing to be available for the experience that calls for our total concentration. And that experience is simply to be wholly open to the experience of Jesus.

People who look at meditation from the outside find it very difficult to understand this. They see it as anti-intellectual. They even see it – religious people have said this to me – as a process of making yourself a cabbage. If they do not understand it is because it is very hard to understand the process of reduction outside of the experience. But it is a process that, when experienced, brings us to the moment of pure truth, the moment of full awareness. Once we are wholly open to that moment we go through the barriers of the limitations of our own consciousness and enter the expansion, the infinite expansiveness of the consciousness of Jesus.

So you must understand that saying the mantra is this process of concentration. It is a process whereby we become available for the *one thing*. And the one thing is everything. The one thing is the only thing. The only thing is God. All of us are unmindful of this. All of us live our lives at various levels of surface distraction and superficial preoccupations. But however distracted we may be, however preoccupied we may be with the immediacy of the day that we have to confront, that substratum of truth, of reality that we call God, is always there. All we have to do is to realize it in order to realize our own potential in him. We are able to realize that we are not condemned to be encapsulated within the limits of our own consciousness but that the invitation for every one of us is to go far beyond self-consciousness to consciousness. The wonder that Christian theology proclaims is that the way of this, the truth of this and the life of this is Jesus. And the great proclamation of the early Church is that he lives in our hearts.

The German mystic, Silesius, reflecting upon the feast of the Nativity, said that it may be that Jesus was born in Bethlehem but that will be of no avail to us, unless he is born in our hearts. There is the whole purpose of Christian meditation, that we *accept* the freedom that the Incarnation has achieved for each of us. To accept it, we have to follow in the way of Jesus. We have to be reduced to the single activity of being; being the person we are called to be and being that person fully. Being who we are means accepting the gift of our creation by God, accepting the gift of our redemption by Jesus and accepting fully the gift of the Spirit, the Holy Spirit dwelling in our hearts. For this Trinitarian acceptance we must turn from everything that is less than the fullness of the Godhead. We must concentrate and we must be concentrated. We must be reduced to nothing so that we may pass through, to become all. The feast of the Nativity is the feast of the reduction of God to man, so that many may enter into Godliness.

Never lose sight of the practicality of meditation. The practicality of it is that each of us has a precise personal task. Each of us has to accept a definite priority in our lives, to put the first thing first. To meditate every morning and every evening is to do this, to make the search for peace, for love, for fullness of life, for fullness of consciousness, our first priority. We can be tempted by the poetry of it all, by the sublime theology of it, merely to admire from the distance. But the invitation is to enter in, to taste and see how wonderful the Lord is. The Incarnation has made the absolute absolutely clear and universally simple:

> For all alike have sinned, and all alike are deprived of the divine splendour, and all alike are justified by God's free grace alone, through His act of liberation in the person of Christ Jesus. (Rom. 3:23–4)

This is the faith our meditation is founded on; entering into that liberty, accepting that act of liberation and being made utterly free. Passing beyond all limitation, we are still, as we become one with God, in total harmony with him. That is the purpose of our meditation. This is the way and the time is now.

Focus on the Real

It is the purpose of all religion to focus our attention on the divine centre and to enlighten our attention with the knowledge that this centre is the source of all love, of all life. What our religious tradition has to teach us is that it is only by contact with and by contemplation on, this divine centre that man is able to become truly himself. In other words, it is only by focusing on the divine that we can get ourselves in focus.

The search which all religion is supposed to guide is the pursuit of what is real. All true religion is concerned with reality and the wisdom that proves the authenticity of religion is simply the gift of distinguishing between illusion and reality. Wisdom is gained by focusing our whole being, our whole attention, on the divine centre. This is the centre of consciousness that is to be found at the same time in our own hearts and utterly beyond us in the depth of God. It is this very act of focusing that leads us to wisdom and so to the knowledge of what is important in life. This knowledge is not static. It constantly empowers us in all the different situations of life to be able to distinguish what is serious and what is essential from what is trivial or frivolous; to distinguish what is passing from what is enduring. Wisdom is the capacity to focus on the real and to reject illusion, or at least to identify illusion as illusion: as trivial, passing, shallow and two-dimensional. The truly spiritual man or woman is the person who has focal depth, who can see things in their interdependent relationships because everything is seen in its relation to the divine centre. We *need* this wisdom and we need it absolutely if we are to live our lives fully, sincerely, earnestly and lovingly. Above all, to live life lovingly we must be in contact with love at the source of our being.

The tradition that I speak about is one that invites us all to enter this wisdom and it teaches us that to enter it we must learn how to become recollected. We must *collect* ourselves together. We must become mindful, remember who we are and where we are and why we are. We need to find a peace within ourselves and a peace in our lives. This peace is a mindfulness, a recollection that will enable us to commence this focusing on the divine centre, the centre from which everything flows and unto which everything flows. Meditation is getting into harmony with that great flow of life from him, with him, to him.

One of the things that we must clearly understand is that meditation, this pursuit of wisdom and love, must take place in an entirely ordinary, natural way. Meditation must be built into the ordinary fabric of everyday life. We must learn to see the whole of life shot through with the divine, in harmony with the divine. We must also understand that it is our destiny to enter this divine harmony, to be in harmony with God. It is not a question of trying to fit a bit of spirituality into our lives. The spiritual quest, the permanent spiritual invitation is getting our lives, ourselves, into permanent focus with ultimate truth, ultimate goodness. Not in any self-important or exploitative way but in a very simple, childlike way. It is by being still, by paying attention and by becoming mindful of the one who loves us. To be fit for the great tasks in life we must learn to be faithful in humble tasks. Meditation is a very simple and very humble pilgrimage that prepares us for this focusing of our lives on the divine centre. Our lives are nourished by the spiritual sap, the energy rising from the root of all being. The invitation that each of us has received is to find out who we are, to discover the destiny that we have, to go beyond the limitations of our separate selves and to be united with the one who is all in all. In that going beyond ourselves, we find ourselves. And we find our unlimited capacity for development, for liberty, for love.

We must be careful of the superlatives! We must be careful of our own enthusiasm because if we use too many superlatives we can forget the humility of the task, the ordinariness of the way. The ordinariness is simply that every morning of our lives and every evening of our lives, we settle down to recollect ourselves. We become mindful, we turn ourselves in the direction of the divine centre and focus ourselves. We do so by the simple expedient of saying our word. We banish all the images that can build a wall between ourselves and reality, by breaking through all the symbols and allowing the pure, brilliant light of reality, the clear light of God's Spirit 'shining', as St Paul puts it, in our hearts, to become *the* supreme reality for us. This task is not too hard for us. We will not have to travel over the sea to find it. We do not have to ask others to do it for us. This reality is very near us. It is in our hearts *if only* we will take the trouble to *seek first* the Kingdom of God, the Kingdom that is in our hearts. It is the reign of God that Jesus himself has established in our hearts and that requires simple fidelity. It is, among other things, faithfulness to common sense; the common sense that tells us we must return constantly to drink, and to drink deeply, at this fountain of life. Drinking deeply there, everything in our lives comes into focus as a consequence. Once we are focused on that divine centre nothing in life or death is unclear.

St Paul has a wonderful description of this experience:

> Therefore, my brothers, I implore you by God's mercy, to offer your very selves to him: a living sacrifice, dedicated and fit for his acceptance, the worship offered by mind and heart. Adapt yourselves no longer to the pattern of this present world, but let your minds be remade and your whole nature thus transformed. Then you will be able to discern the will of God, and to know what is good, acceptable and perfect. (Rom 12:1–2)

This is a wonderful description of meditation. 'Let your minds be remade'. Saying the mantra is, as it were, wiping clean the slate of consciousness so that our consciousness may be filled with the knowledge of the love of God. It is the fullness of his love that transforms us. What transforms our whole nature also enlightens us so that, being transformed, we seek what is good and perfect and the will of God is clear.

Trying to Keep God Happy

Today we live, on the whole, in a very unstable world. Part of the problem is that we ourselves are not personally very rooted and as a result there are so many unstable, uncertain, insecure people around. The early Christian vision saw life as being triumphantly rooted. St Paul constantly speaks of our lives as Christians as being *rooted* 'in Christ', *grounded* in him, *founded* in him. But history has since subjected us to so many more social pressures. For example, the pressure of fashion which begets the desire to conform to the external image that people expect of us. Whether that image is itself conformist or non-conformist, it makes us unwilling slaves of the desire to please. So often we cannot be ourselves because we do not experience ourselves as rooted in any real, solid identity of our own choice or making. Of course cause and effect are confused in such a world. When the world is unstable, it means poor relationships. If we are uncertain of ourselves, then it is very difficult for us to go out to meet others, to love others. And because we do not know what we think about ourselves, we are always wondering what other people are thinking about us. Because we seem to ourselves so insignificant, we seek fame or envy those who find it. But the Christian view offers a very different understanding of what it means to be human, even today.

St Paul's idea of living our lives 'in union' with Christ means that we are unshakeably rooted in reality. As St John Climacus put it, 'we care not whether the world praises us or whether the world criticizes us' because we are rooted in what is, in the one who is. Because we are rooted in love, all we care for is love. We are not concerned with trying to project the right image of ourselves and, above all, we are not trying to make ourselves 'acceptable' to others. The truth that we know, and know with absolute certainty is that we are 'accepted'. The truth, and this is a truth open for us all to discover, is that we are infinitely lovable. And not only infinitely lovable, but infinitely loved. Again, though, we must experience that for ourselves. Our modern scepticism betrays the inability to trust. Underlying that is the erosion of belief that is caused by lack of personal experience. When the thread between belief and experience gets too thin we feel, quite appropriately, at breaking point. We must, therefore, know our real, lovable value with personal certainty born of experience that flowers in our own hearts. This is what the pilgrimage of meditation leads us to. When we meditate we fix our whole attention on what is and what is essential. The essence of what it means to be alive is that we are in union with our creator. The essence of the Christian vision is that the Spirit of God dwells in our heart. It is a spirit of compassion, of understanding, of forgiveness and of love. In meditation we *experience* ourselves as loved, forgiven, accepted – not just as barely acceptable. When we know this in relation to God we do not have to go around making ourselves acceptable to others.

Religious people have often become very confused by thinking that religion demands that they 'placate' God or keep him happy or distract him from punishing them. So religious people tend to get too busy with their ceremonies and liturgies. But we must also learn to be still and to be rooted in the knowledge that we need neither placate God nor distract him. We need only respond to his infinite love. We respond by total attention, by total stillness, not thinking of his love but by being open to it; not thinking of his mercy, but receiving it. The one thing we must understand is that in the time of meditation we need not think about anything. This is the time of the day for total attention, for total openness, for total love. The Christian experience is, in essence, a certain knowledge that God is love and that he lives in our hearts. Our call, therefore, is more than to dialogue with him, it is to be in union with him. To be one with him, each of us must come to the fullness of our own created oneness. Each of us must experience our own harmony in order that we may be in total harmony with him. The Christian way is a way where each of us is made whole by becoming completely stable, completely rooted in truth, in love, in goodness, in justice. In fact, in God.

Meditation is simply the time for realizing that rootedness. When we sit down we enter into the stability of being which bears fruit in a magnanimous and unshakeable confidence. 'Who shall separate us from the love of Christ?' No power on earth or in heaven, or any that we could imagine. Absorb the confidence of these words of St Paul's Letter to the Colossians.

> Therefore, since Jesus was delivered to you as Christ and Lord, live your lives in union with Him. Be rooted in him; be built in him; be consolidated in the faith you were taught; let your hearts overflow with thankfulness. . . For it is in Christ that the complete being of the Godhead dwells embodied, and in him you have been brought to completion. (Col. 2:6–7,9)

Meditation is simply pure openness to that wholeness of perfection which is ours in Christ.

Questions and Answers

Q: Is meditation the same as contemplation?
A: I think that meditation and contemplation can both be understood as journeys. *Meditate* means to be in the centre and *contemplate* means to be in the temple with the Lord. Both of them are, therefore, also states as well as processes and both are journeys into the experience of the mystical state. But mysticism is not a word I care to use too much. As you know, they say if you go in for the mystical life it begins in mist and ends in schism. It's not a word that I think is particularly useful in talking or thinking of prayer. I think the essential thing to understand is the universal relevance and simplicity of the contemplative tradition. We like to analyse and to categorize our experience and perhaps there is a place for that some way down the road. But I think the essential thing to understand and to experience is the sheer simplicity of saying the mantra. Saying the mantra (which is *meditation*) is to enter into total silence, to be totally grounded in your being, in the being of God (which is *contemplation*). It is not very valuable to argue about the vocabulary for describing the experience until you have really begun to enter the experience personally.

Q: You seem to be downplaying the sensory part of human existence. What about the senses?
A: I don't think we're trying to downplay them. I think, in fact, that meditation is an experience of the total integration of body and spirit. That's why, for example, I stress so much the importance of actually sitting still, physically. Your physical posture is of great importance. What you will find in the daily life that flows out of meditating is that the whole of your

sensory awareness, your bodily life, becomes integrated with your spirit. It isn't a downplaying of that wholeness. But there *is* a downplaying, if you like, of indulging the senses or of seeing the ultimate meaning of life through the sensory dimension alone. Meditation is about a deeper commitment to humanity through a deeper awareness in all your being, including your sensory perception. And so I think you'll find that through meditation you see things and hear things and touch things and smell things, as you have never done before. I think that you'll notice as a result of meditating, how deepened and refined all your perceptions become, sensory and mental. So I don't think there is a downplaying of the body at all. Unless you mean during the actual moment of meditation. Because at that time, of course, one is being totally still in body as well as mind. But in your life in general – and meditation is not to be seen as divorced from your life in general, but wholly integrated with it – you'll see that gradually the whole of your sensory perception is deepened and refined. Don't think that stillness is static. Don't think that renunciation is rejection.

Q: The mantra seems such a tiny thing to do and yet has such an effect on the way we see life.
A: Yes, I think that's absolutely right. And I think, as evidently you have discovered, you *can* only discover this great smallness through experience. The mantra is or seems so small and yet turns us right around. It's like the saying of Jesus in the gospel; the mustard seed is the smallest of all seeds and yet when planted, becomes a mighty bush and the birds of the air come and nest in it. The mantra is just the same. It's a very small word, it's a tiny seed of faith but it does root you beyond ephemera, beyond things that are just passing away, but to live them rooted in what is eternal. And that's what the mantra does. It roots you in that eternal reality which we call God.

Q: Father John, I have a couple of questions that relate to the process of meditation as opposed to the goal. You mentioned again in your prelude to the meditation tonight that we must try to eliminate *all* images – images of God, images of ourselves, images of other people. Is it *psychologically* possible for the human mind to eliminate all images?

A: Well, that's a subtle question, but I think the answer must be that it has to be possible *if* total union is possible. Because I think that when there is total union with ultimate reality there cannot be any supervening image. It would seem to me to be a logical impossibility. So I think the answer to your question is that if total union is possible, then it *is* possible to go beyond all images.

Q: Okay then, my second question is this: the mantra itself is a special kind of word. There are, in other circumstances other special kinds of words: for example, a hypnotist might suggest to a patient, to repeat a word, and the immediate aim in repeating the word would be to go into some kind of deep relaxation. The ultimate aim might be something else, say to give up smoking. What is the *immediate* objective of saying the mantra?

A: I think the immediate objective is to bring you to silence. This is what most people will experience when they begin to meditate for the first time. Most people find, not everyone, that very early on they do come to a most extraordinary silence and peacefulness. But then as they proceed this gives way to a very distracted state of being, and they begin to feel during this stage, well, this is hard, perhaps meditation is not for me. I have no talent for it, all I seem to get now when I meditate is more and more distractions. But I think that is the crucial moment to persevere. The *ultimate* aim of meditation is what motivates you then, and that aim is to bring you to a *total* silence. As I've probably said to you before, it has to be a silence that is entirely unself-conscious and so as soon as you realize, consciously, that you are in this silence and that it is all very marvellous, you must begin to say your mantra again immediately. That trains you in the generosity of not trying to possess the fruit of your meditation. It is very difficult for people today to accept this teaching of the mantra because most people in our society go into something so that they can experience the experience.

Meditation is different from that. It is an entry into pure experience.

Now the way that the ancient wisdom expressed this is expressed in the saying that 'the monk who knows that he is praying, is not praying. The monk who does not know he is praying, is praying'. So say your mantra until you come to total silence. You may be in that silence for a split second. You may be in it for a minute, you may be in it for twenty minutes. But as soon as you realize you're in it, start saying the mantra again. And don't try to make that silence happen. I think that's another hazard – that we want to make progress. We want to get some sort of verification that the whole business of saying the mantra for five years is going to be worth it. At that stage, especially, you must resist the temptation to try to possess the fruits of meditation. We must just meditate and say the mantra and when you realize you are not saying it, say it again.

But it's those moments of pure silence that are the moments of revelation. I don't often speak of this because it would be disastrous to try to confect that experience. And no one who is seriously listening to this teaching should ever attempt to confect the experience. What you must do is say your mantra and be content to say it. Be humble to say it. Be simple to say it. The gift of prayer, of pure prayer, the gift of pure contemplation, the gift of pure silence is an absolute *gift*. It is never something that we can, as it were, earn or twist God's arm to get. When it is given, we accept it with joy and then we say our mantra again. I think that's the distinction between immediate and ultimate aims. Does that answer your question?

Q: You recommend a specific thirty-minute period for meditation but it is distracting to have to keep thinking or checking on the time.

A: It is probably better for that reason to have a timer of some kind. People use all sorts of devices. Some people, for example, take a forty-five minute casette and 'record' on it a half hour of silence, and at the end of the silence record some quiet music. So you press the button when you start to meditate and when the music comes on, you know that your half hour is up.

91

Other people use a kind of kitchen timer. You would want to use something that has a fairly gentle ping, or you may give yourself a bit of a shock at the end. It is an important practical question to know how to time it, because the really important thing is the discipline of meditating. Choose a specific time, twenty, twenty-five or ideally thirty minutes. Then meditate for that time. When you are starting the temptation is, if things are 'going well' and you are approaching cloud nine, to prolong the meditation. Or, if things are 'going badly' – such phrases have no real meaning but that is what we feel when we are beginning – you say, 'Well, this is a total waste of time, might as well cut this out and go and cut the lawn or jog.' The important quality is to stick at it, whether it is going well or going badly or however it is 'going'. There is only one way for it to go, actually, and that is for you to say your mantra from beginning to end.

Q: What's the meaning of the mantra?
A: The meaning of the mantra which is in Aramaic, a language that Jesus spoke, is 'Come Lord'. But I don't recommend you to think about the meaning when you're saying it. Say it simply as a word, as a sound. Because, if you start thinking of the meaning, then you are immediately likely to drift off into images of what you're thinking about or of yourself in relation to it. The essence of meditating is to have no thoughts, no images.

Q: What is the function of the mantra?
A: The function of the mantra is, basically, to bring you to silence, to take you beyond thought, imagination, ratiocination and self-consciousness.

Q: It's a way to clear your mind?
A: Yes, you could certainly put it that way. Saying the mantra, I think, is very much what William Blake meant when he talked of 'cleansing the doors of your perception'. It's very much a clarifying of your consciousness. But you have to be careful about too strong images, even in thinking about the mantra,

because otherwise your temptation is to say at the end of your meditation, well, how much more clarification have I got this time? Whereas, you want to try and approach meditation in the least self-conscious way possible. And that's the purpose – to bring you to the silence of direct consciousness.

Q: Does meditation affect the way we experience goodness and evil more as reality and illusion?
A: I think so. I think that the key point about reality and illusion is that the illusion is illusion because it has no reality in the divine perspective. It can of course seem very real at the time in your own perspective. If somebody plays a really evil trick on you, then that seems vividly real to you. Say someone steals your wallet when you're going out to do some shopping. At the moment you discover it, it seems very, very real. And it even seems real to the guy who stole it. He's now got fifty dollars more than he had when he started. But in the divine perspective, his moment of glory is over and so even is your painful moment of confronting the truth of finding that you're fifty bucks short. You go on to face the unpleasant truth that someone with a certain propensity to evil has caused you unprovoked harm. If you are to deal with its evil, you have to avoid judging the whole thing from your self-centredness. Only then can you forgive. All of that – from both centres of concern – that's *all* reality. It's the whole reality from the divine perspective in which every point of view is contained. I think that's the difference between illusion and reality: that reality has an eternal all-inclusive significance; illusion is a flash in the pan on a particular stove. Meditation detaches us from our tendency to believe that our point of view is the only or truest one. It does this by teaching us to give up our own thoughts and ideas entirely, in favour of the all-inclusive reality of God.

Q: But we hurt when we are done harm to.
A: We do, yes. Our hurt seems *totally* real, but it isn't. It is part of reality. Our commitment to total reality, in answer to your question, is something we are beginning now. It comes to total fulfilment in the Beatific Vision.

Q: Isn't this really all a very Eastern concept. 'Well, it's an illusion, my dear friend, that you're suffering'. It's an illusion that there are millions of people starving but they will be fulfilled later. How far can you step out of that and say, well it's illusion?

A: Well, it's *totally* real as long as we are materialists. But if you look at it and say, what is the significance of this, then you begin to understand what is real in it and what is illusion in it. I think the problem is that we are all brought up in such a materialistic atmosphere that if someone has stolen your wallet or even your life it seems like the ultimate reality. If we attribute total reality to changing human experience it's very difficult to believe that only God is real, and that everything else is real only in so far as it is a participation in his reality. Evil cannot participate in his reality but the finite can. Therefore, we *can* open our hearts in compassion to human suffering in God. To put it neatly, the hand that delivers the blow is acting in an unreal way. The hand that brings comfort is acting in a real, a Godlike, way. God is not indifferent. God is good. God is love. It is difficult to understand through concepts, but experience of suffering and compassion, of evil and good, clarifies it. Someone once said to W. B. Yeats, 'Mr Yeats, when I read some of your poems, I can't understand that they mean. Could you tell me what they mean?' And Yeats replied, in effect, 'Perhaps I *can* tell you what they mean. But I know that for me, they are supremely real. All I have to convey to you by my poetry, if I can, is that for me this is supremely important. Perhaps I *can't* explain to you what it means (because maybe *I* don't even know what it means) but I am certain that it's important'. Much of Christian theology has to operate at that level. I think that's the importance of meditating; it gives us this, if you like, *instinct* for what is right, or a perspective on what is right in the eternal vision of God. We will only know fully at the moment of the Beatific Vision. Seeing God means seeing everything as he sees it and knows it.

Q: You say we find the light of Christ in our depth. Do we have to face darkness on the way?

A: It isn't really possible to say very much that is useful about meditation because you have to use words and analogies, like light and depth and darkness. They are metaphors, drawn from experiences that are themselves metaphors for purer experience. But I think that, in a way, depth does also mean darkness. It does mean rootedness, and it's by passing beyond the superficial levels of our being, into our depths that we find our roots in the mystery that is Christ. I think you are right, that probably the only way to pass to that depth is through darkness. But it is once you are rooted in that reality, that you are, as it were, able to see the light in the roots and to rise up into the light. For the fullness of the Christian life you do need the commitment made in the darkness, which is an aspect of faith. You do need to go down to full rootedness in Christ, when you are in the darkness of 'no experience', of nothing to reassure you. But then, as the life in that rootedness brings you to growth, you grow into or up into the light of Christ. Then it is not a matter of 'nothing's happening' but of 'there's nothing that isn't happening'. But the way to the light is through the dark. Let it be dark, therefore. Don't try to take flash pictures, to analyse or 'understand' it. In a similar sense, the way to listen is through silence. Silence seems very negative until you realize that it's absolutely necessary for all listening, for all hearing. And the darkness of the depth is necessary for that rootedness in the light.

Q: Is it Christ who makes it possible for us to act on this?

A: I think that he really does make the difference. The leap of faith, the leap into the dark, does require the absolute trust we have in him. You have to make the leap trusting that he will be there to catch you, as it were. The difference he makes is what the Letter to the Hebrews describes: that he has established the way and has leapt before us. And so the way right over is now possible. It's made. The way over is the spirit of Christ. That is the profoundest difference that you could possibly imagine. There's no greater difference between something having been done and not having been done. Because it has been done, we have every reason to make the leap, every confidence in making it. Faith is the conviction, hope is the confidence and love is the result. That's again why meditation is so important, because it's so necessary to discover from your own experience that love does cast out all fear. Christ's achievement is to have overcome that fear in himself, on behalf of us, and to have shared the love that resulted with us, to cast out our fear. It's not enough to leave all that just at the level of theological proposition or religious poetry. The invitation to each of us is to discover that as supreme reality. The way is to leap ourselves and this is the way of the mantra.

Summary of the Teaching

Learning to meditate and learning what meditation has to teach us are both different kinds of learning from what we are used to. We are not learning anything 'new' in our usual understanding of novelty. We are *re-learning* something known in childhood and lost before we could maturely integrate it. We are *unlearning* much, conditioned by our education and training, that is inadequate for a fully developed life. What we are learning by this process of re-learning and unlearning is something too simple and direct for us to understand, except in and through experience. We are too complex and self-conscious for the experience when we begin. Some teaching, not only by example (the best teaching) but also by words and ideas, is needed to keep us on the way that prepares us for the 'magisterial experience' itself. Let me try to summarize this most simple of teachings, the essential elements of meditation. Let me begin by placing us in the context of the essential Christian teaching in Scripture. St Paul here is reflecting upon the potential we all have for a richer and fuller life, for a life rooted in the mystery of God.

I kneel in prayer to the Father, from whom every family in heaven and on earth takes its name, that out of the treasures of his glory he may grant you strength and power through his Spirit in your inner being, that through faith Christ may dwell in your hearts in love. With deep roots and firm foundations, may you be strong to grasp, with all God's people, what is the breadth and length and height and depth of the love of Christ, and to know it, though it is beyond knowledge. So may you attain to fullness of being, the fullness of God himself. (Eph. 3:14–19)

This is a marvellously comprehensive description of the destiny that each of us has, as Christians, as human beings. Our destiny and call is to come to a fullness of being which is the fullness of God himself. In other words, each of us is summoned to an unlimited, infinite development through the way of faith and love, as we leave the narrowness of our own ego behind, and enter into the ever-expanding mystery of God's own self.

The one quality we need to begin is courage. Beginning to meditate is like drilling for oil in the desert. The surface is so dry and so dusty, that you have to take on faith the findings of the geologists who tell you that, deep within this dry earth, there is a great source of power. When we begin to meditate for the first time we cannot help expecting something to happen, that we will now see some vision, now come to some deeper knowledge. But nothing happens. Persevering past this stage, one of many hurdles our faith will encounter, leads us to see that quietly at work in the heart of our faith is love. When we see this, that it is not only by faith that we proceed but by faith and love, then we have really begun. Through this faith Christ dwells within us in love. His indwelling is the constant companionship of the teacher. Our initiatory courage has led us to find our teacher.

But it really is because 'nothing happens' that you can be sure that you are on the right path, the path of simplicity, of poverty, of an empowering surrender. Jesus has told us that his Spirit is to be found in our hearts. Meditating is uncovering this truth as a present reality deep within ourselves at the centre of our lives. The Spirit that we are invited to discover in our heart is the power source that enriches every aspect and part of our life. The Spirit is the eternal Spirit of life and the almighty Spirit of love. The call of Christians is not to be half-alive, which means being half-dead, but to be *fully* alive, alive with the *dynamos* of the Spirit, with the power and energy that St Paul speaks of, and that is continually flowing in our hearts. To liberate this power is to be liberated ourselves. Liberty follows, if we will undertake the discipline to make our way to it, day by day. The way of meditation is simplicity itself. We only have to begin simply and to continue simply. It is essential to tread the path, to be on the way, each day of our lives. Because the Spirit is continually flowing in us, carrying us with it towards God, we must be continually uncovering it.

A very effective sign of this continuity of presence is the physical stillness we discipline ourselves to adopt during each meditation. It is something we need to learn, to relearn as we unlearn our conditioned restlessness. We simply place our body on the cushion, in the chair, and we leave it there, totally devoted to the work of meditation. This is the first step away from egoism and from our compulsive concern with ourselves as we open our consciousness to what is beyond ourselves, the limitless reality that expands our spirit into an unpredictably generous, selfless love. The challenge that each of us has to face is to go beyond where we are now, to go further. We are pilgrims and we therefore have to make progress. The progression depends upon our willingness to grow, to develop, beyond ourselves, into the profound and generous life of God. So to begin, we sit still.

Then, closing our eyes gently, we begin to recite our mantra. To meditate all we have to do is to say the word from the beginning to the end. Do not think about what you are doing, what you are not doing. Do not think about yourself. Do not wonder, 'Is this a complete waste of time? Is this going to do me any good? What am I going to get out of this?' All those thoughts must fall away, must be abandoned. They will cease to trouble you if you persevere with the mantra, deepening your faith, liberating the power of the Spirit's love. Meditation is continually bringing us to a state of undivided consciousness where we become one with the one who is one. Our growing unity, within ourselves and with God is the process that under-lies our sense that we, or rather, the life lived within us, is becoming more profound, more generous, more alive. Meditation asks of us however that we are utterly practical in our commitment, in our spiritual commitment.

The call, the destiny that you hear St Paul assign to each of us, is not a call just to enter into the religious moments in our busy schedules, into a *bit* of spiritual richness. It is to enter fully and utterly, without reserve, without counting the cost, into the truth that empowers each of us to be fully human, truly self-confident, which means confident to love and to be loved. Again, we must remember that we are not talking about some elitist or esoteric doctrine. This call, this destiny, is within the reach of each of us. All we have to do is to begin to commit ourselves to the journey, to the practice. And the practice of this tradition – and do not let anything mislead you on this – is to say the word from the beginning to the end with growing fidelity. This truth of our destiny is not only accessible to us, it is the ground on which all reality stands. To come to this reality we have to learn to be simple, to be still, to be silent. These are the elements of prayer and to pray is to be attentive – attentive to what is the supreme reality of God's presence, his love, within our own hearts. So we must learn to stop thinking about ourselves. We must learn simply to be, which means to be fully attentive in the presence of God, in the presence of the one who is, and who is the ground of our being and all being. We need have no fear as we set out, as we leave self behind and set out to meet the other. We need have no doubt or fear. The Spirit in our hearts, the Spirit to which we open in meditation is the Spirit of compassion, of gentleness, of forgiveness, of total acceptance, the Spirit of love.

For our lives to be fully human we need to encounter the Spirit of love within ourselves. It is not a journey just for spiritual experts. It is a journey for everyone who would live their lives to the full. Who was St Paul writing to when he wrote these words?

> I pray that your inward eyes may be illumined, so that you may know what is the hope to which he calls you, what the wealth and glory of the share he offers you . . . and how vast the resources of his power open to us who trust in him. (Eph. 1:18–19)

Meditation is the great way of trust. We sit down, we sit still, we say our mantra with growing fidelity and trust our whole selves utterly to God. We do that every morning and every evening of our lives and thus we learn to live out of that trust, to live out of the love that faith reveals and liberates.

The Path that Forgets Itself

St Paul is the quintessential Christian teacher, a passionate disciple and brother. This is his concern and his prayer for those he was guiding in the faith: 'May the Lord direct your hearts towards God's love and the steadfastness of Christ' (2 Th. 3:5). I think this is the purpose of meditation, too, that our hearts are directed towards God's love. The steadfastness of Christ is the faithfulness that we require if we are to stay on this path of conversion, the path that is constantly forgetful of itself, moving out beyond self to God. God's love, that St Paul speaks of, is reached through the steadfastness we find in Christ. Love involves a total acceptance of the other, an other-directedness that is entirely unconditional. It is an acceptance of the other that is so total that the self is lost. For such a lover there is only the other. And the extraordinary paradox of love is that in that state of selflessness, where the self is lost and forgotten, we find the self. We find our self almost for the first time with an original wonder. The new element is that now we find our self loved. And there is a real sense in which we can say that unless we are loved we can never find our self.

Now consider this in relation to meditation. The saying of the mantra is an act of pure selflessness. Every time we say the mantra we renounce, we leave behind, our own thoughts, our own concerns, our own hopes, our own fears. In losing these properties or possessions of the self we lose the self. In saying the mantra we become, as the Zen phrase puts it 'the eye that sees but that cannot see itself'. A person meditating is a person looking straight ahead. His vision becomes clarified because none of the distorting images of egoism can in any way refract the pure light of God which both enters and emerges from the eye of the heart. Meditation is the way of love because its meaning and purpose is communion. But we simply cannot find adequate language to talk about meditation and that is why the Buddhist vocabulary, for example, or the sayings of Jesus, are so paradoxical to minds used to the half-truths of mundane experience. Nevertheless it is a true and necessary paradox that we must lose ourselves, we must leave our self absolutely behind in order to find our self.

The word *communion* expresses as perfectly as any the experience of meditation: that we are in a common union. Jesus and ourselves united with the Father. The way of meditation is a way of knowing reality simply because it is only by this most complete and undifferentiated union with the Creator that we can live fully out of our own roots. To live fully is to be conscious of our origin and so live fully out of the power of God. For this awareness we need to be steadfast. We need that steel in the spine that will enable us to return day after day to meditation; not concerned so much with progress or enlightenment or success but with the faithful, humble return to our task. In meditation as Christians our hearts are directed towards God's love. Each of us has to discover and then to remember, knowing it with absolute clarity and certainty, that we are infinitely loveable and infinitely loved. We must know it, not just as an intellectual proposition but with experiential knowledge, in our own hearts. It is the most important knowledge there is for any of us and that is why meditation is so important. By meditating we can fasten our minds and hearts upon the essential fact of history, the pivotal knowledge of the human mind, that God is love. It is what Jesus came to proclaim, and yet to do more than proclaim it. He came to establish this knowledge in your heart as in mine. To be a Christian is to live out of that conviction but how can we live out of it unless we know it? That is why we return to the humble task of saying our mantra every morning and every evening.

The man or woman of prayer is a man or woman in communion, in daily communion with love, in deepening communion with God. So do not allow yourselves to be side-tracked by any sort of materialistic canons of judgement. Do not bother about success. Do not bother about making progress or achieving results in your meditation. The only thing to be concerned about is to meditate on a daily basis and to say your word as best you can. Remember saying the word is like seeing with the eye looking straight ahead, not seeing itself but seeing the vision ahead. The vision is the infinity of God's love. The vision is our own meaning and value, as we are made real in the light of love. And this vision is for everyone, everyone, that is, who would be fully human, fully themselves, fully loving.

May the Lord direct your hearts towards God's love and the steadfastness of Christ. (2 Thess. 3:5)

Growing Point

This is the last time we shall meet together in this house[1]. It has meant a great deal to us in the community here to have been so greatly encouraged and supported by the faithfulness and perseverance of each one of you, some of you for almost three years. The place where we have experienced friendship is always important and we shall miss meeting with you in these intimate surroundings here. But life moves on, on our pilgrimage, and we must all grow up. So we look forward to meeting you again in our new house on Pine Avenue.

As this evening does mark a certain watershed in our relationship, I would like to reflect with you on what is the basic thing that we learn from meditation. The important thing about meditation is that it is a learning process. It is a process where we enter ever more deeply, ever more richly into *the* mystery. I think that what we all discover from our own experience is that God is Spirit. God is the breath of life. God is presence and he is present deep within our being, in our hearts. If only we persevere we discover that in the power of his Spirit each one of us is regenerated, renewed, recreated so that we become a new creation in him. 'I have poured out my Spirit upon this people', said the prophet Ezekiel. And the Spirit is the presence of power, the power of love. Meditation teaches us that this is the foundational wisdom 'on which to build life and true religion. What we discover is that we can only live our lives fully if we are *always* open to this mysterious presence

[1] This is the last talk given at the first home of the Montreal community on Vendôme Avenue. In November 1980 it moved to Pine Avenue. See John Main, *Letters from the Heart* (New York 1982), *The Present Christ* (London and New York 1985).

of the Spirit, and *always* open to the presence more profoundly. That is the pilgrimage we enter upon every time we sit down to meditate. We open our minds, our hearts, our consciousness more permanently to the ultimate reality that is, that is now, that is here.

What is the basis of the Christian mystery? It is surely that the beyond is in our midst, that absolute reality is here and now. The Christian faith teaches that by being open to the mystery of this reality we are taken out of ourselves, beyond ourselves, into the absolute mystery which is God. God is how we transcend self. We transcend all limitation by simple openness to the All who is now. The great awakening to the mystery is the Kingdom of heaven and the Kingdom of heaven is now. It is established by Jesus and proclaimed by his own words, 'The Kingdom of God is upon you. Repent and believe in the gospel'. To repent means simply to turn in the direction of God. Repenting is turning not so much away from ourselves (for that keeps us still tied to our own centre) but beyond ourselves. This means not rejecting ourselves but finding our marvellous potential as we come into full harmony with God. This awareness of potential is the positive basis of Christianity and so, for a Christian, the central concern is not self, nor is it sin. The central reality is God and love and, as far as we are concerned, growth in God's love. Growth consists both in our openness to his love for us and in the response we make by returning that love.

'Repent and believe in the gospel.' Believing the gospel simply means being committed to openness to our potential. Each one of us possesses unknown potential in the extraordinary plan of personal salvation and this is what Jesus discloses to each of us in the stillness of our heart as we undertake the journey of silence and of absolute commitment to silence and pure openness every morning and every evening. What he reveals is that we are created for love, for freedom, for transcendent meaning, for fulfilment; and we realize it all by entering the mystery of the Kingdom that is upon us. That mystery is now unfolded by the generous gift of Christ.

St Paul proclaims this event in the last words of his Letter to the Romans:

> To him who has power to make your standing sure, according to the Gospel I brought you and the proclamation of Jesus Christ, according to the revelation of that divine secret kept in silence for long ages but now disclosed, and through prophetic scriptures by eternal God's command made known to all nations, to bring them to faith and obedience – to God who alone is wise, through Jesus Christ, be glory for endless ages! Amen. (Rom 16:25–7)

The Kingdom *is* established. Faith and obedience teach us to realize it. Remember the practicalities of the work of realization. Learn to be silent and to love silence. When we meditate we don't look for messages or signs, or phenomena. Each of us must learn to be humble, patient and faithful. Discipline teaches us to be still, and by stillness we learn to empty our heart of everything that is not God, for he requires all the room that our heart has to offer. This emptiness is the purity of heart we develop by saying our mantra with absolute fidelity. The mystery is absolute truth, absolute love and so too our response must be absolute. We respond absolutely by becoming simple. The power of such simplicity is evident in these other words of St Paul to the Corinthians:

> As for me, brothers, when I came to you, I declared the attested truth of God without display of fine words or wisdom. . . I came before you weak. . . The word I spoke, the gospel I proclaimed, did not sway you with subtle arguments; it carried conviction by spiritual power, so that your faith might be built not upon human wisdom but upon the power of God. (1 Cor. 2:1, 3–5)

In the simplicity of our meditation we prepare our hearts to be absolutely open to that power.